Jump Start

180 Lessons, Icebreakers, Projects, and Weekend Activities for JUNIOR HIGH

Jump Start

Michael Amodei

AVE MARIA PRESS   Notre Dame, Indiana 46556

© 1998 by Ave Maria Press, Inc.
International Standard Book Number: 0-87793-662-5
Cover and text design by: Brian C. Conley
Printed and bound in the United States of America.

To my mom, a great teacher.

Contents

Introduction

When I was a young guy just out of college I burned both ends of the candle quite frequently, and not just on weekends either.

During the week I was a full-time teacher at a Catholic grammar school. In a departmentalized setup I taught math and religion to sixth, seventh, and eighth graders. In the afternoons I coached CYO sports. On Sunday nights I sometimes helped with the high school youth ministry group. And every Thursday night I taught a scripture class to seventh and eighth graders in the religious education program.

I was a rare bird. I was the one who dared to cross that bridge between the school and religious education. Surely I must have been doing it only to find out which CCD kids had been marking on and taking things from my regular students' desks.

Actually, I had other motivations. I honestly believed that all the junior high kids in the parish should have times when they could come together. Previously, they met each other only during the week before confirmation at the end of eighth grade. At that time they would attend a one-day "retreat," but no amount of mixers, icebreakers, or assigned small groups could naturally forge a bond between kids in each of these groups.

Why did I want the school and religious ed. kids to come together so badly? Well, the school dances were a dud. Only the usual handful of guys and girls ever came. Also, I wanted to start an after school intramural basketball league. I needed more kids to make both of these activities work.

I didn't think we could just start inviting the religious ed. kids to come to school events and expect them to attend. They barely showed up for the confirmation retreat, which was required. That's when I looked for some neutral ground where kids from both groups would be comfortable to participate even in the midst of all the posturing of prepubescence.

Neutral ground turned out to be a regular Sunday Mass; it became the meeting point. I reserved two pews in the middle of the church where the junior high kids could sit together. They liked the middle because they didn't stand out; they didn't want to be noticed.

At the end of Mass, we met. It wasn't school and it wasn't CCD. Some mixers and icebreakers, a mini-project, a tiny taste of catechesis, and discussion took place. We also had lunch.

After lunch we did something REALLY fun, the kind of fun you can do only on a weekend—like a scavenger hunt, a swim party, a trip to an amusement park, or an afternoon movie. By the way, in case you couldn't guess, it was the fun part that got the kids to come together. Basically, the schedule looked like this, though it can and was adapted to fit the activity we had planned:

> 10:00 Mass
> 11:30 Session
> 12:45 Lunch
> 1:15 Activity
> 4:00 Pick up

We didn't do this every week. In fact, we had only one of these events per month. I held them each second Sunday of the month and called it "Second Sundays" so that the kids and parents could remember the date even if the flier fell off the refrigerator door.

This concept worked well: the religious ed. kids eventually became comfortable enough to attend the school-sponsored events, there were more than enough basketball players for the intramural league, and by confirmation time a real retreat could take place.

This book offers the resources for holding events one Sunday (or Saturday) per month for all of the junior high teens and pre-teens in the parish. There is enough material for three complete years of events without ever repeating one. However, this book can also be used with a variety of youth ministry schedules; it's a helpful supplement to any junior high programming you are already doing. It can be used to reach out to all of the junior high age kids on the parish rolls as a first and ongoing step in keeping this group active and participating during this unique time of their lives.

Some explanations of each of the parts of the Sunday events follow.

The Sunday Mass

The Mass that is part of the Sunday event does not have to be specially designed as a junior high theme Mass. The junior high participants can attend any regular Sunday or Saturday vigil Mass. Most of the time the regular Sunday morning family Mass is most appropriate because it fits well with the rest of the day's schedule. However, occasionally you may have planned an activity—for example, a trip to the amusement park—that will take most of a full day. For those times the participants can attend the Saturday night Mass or an early Sunday morning Mass.

Most junior high students in a parish school or religious education program still attend Sunday Mass with their parents. This is a good habit! Families are not excluded from attending the Mass on junior high day.

Sometimes a parent will say, "But we always go to the eight o'clock Mass. Now you want my child to go to the ten o'clock Mass." Well, this event is not worth causing a family problem. If the family is not able to make an adjustment, so be it. The important thing is that the kid is going to Mass. He or she can join up later with the rest of the programming.

The one regular preparation you will have to make for Mass is to reserve enough pews for all the kids to sit together. Arrange this with the pastor or liturgy coordinator. Try to reserve pews somewhere in the middle of the church. (Remember, they don't like to be noticed.)

Why should the junior high students sit together? There are several reasons:

- They offer a visible presence as a large group and remind the rest of the parish community to pray for them.

- When they know they are somewhat of a "focus," junior high students will not only behave better, but they are also more likely to say and sing the Mass responses than they would if they were sitting with their families.

- You can take mental attendance so that you know that everyone who shows up later for the session and activity was also at Mass.

- Some kids whose families don't attend Mass or some non-Catholic friends of those attending the event will have a place to meet and sit.

You may have some kids who would like to sit with their families. No problem. They can join you later.

The only rule for the session is that in order to participate in the beach trip, bowling contest, dance, or whatever other activity is planned, the person must attend Mass that weekend. Mass is the ticket for entry.

Put it to the kids this way: Eucharist is the most important thing Catholics do. Jesus is present to us in the eucharist, especially in the blessed bread and wine. Catholics also have an obligation to attend Sunday Mass.

After a few months, you may want to work with the liturgy coordinator and plan some more visible ways the junior high participants can be involved in the Mass. For example, a junior high person could be prepared to do a reading or several could bring up the offertory gifts and take the collection. One person could recite a post-communion reflection related to the theme of the Mass. Two or three could be altar servers. These are just a few of the options.

It's always wise to have some adult or high school age chaperones sit amidst the junior high participants at Mass. If a rare behavior problem takes place, the chaperones can deal with it. Usually, the main role of the chaperones will be to lead the participants to the session meeting place after Mass ends.

The Sunday Session

The Sunday session takes place right after Mass. It's best not to allow the participants to mingle with the rest of the community after Mass, given their propensity to scatter. Also, the day's schedule from this point on is tight.

The Sunday session has a theme related to the month it's in. For example, a January theme might focus on Martin Luther King, Jr. and racism or on the baptism of Jesus—that is, holidays and feasts celebrated that month. You can also use the day's readings as a starting point for a theme.

Hold the session in a non-classroom setting. The format of the session should be such that you mix an important lesson amidst icebreakers, activities, projects, and fun. A large semicircle of chairs is the basic room arrangement. Sixth, seventh, and eighth graders are too squirmy to be floor-sitters.

The session is scheduled for about one hour and fifteen minutes. During this time, plenty of movement between different types of facilitation methods and procedures should take place. The only way to keep the participants' minds off lunch and the upcoming activity is to make the session fast-moving and fun. A description and time breakdown of the main parts of the session follows. (Thirty-six complete session plans—three per month—are included in Part I.)

Icebreakers (about 15 minutes) An icebreaker helps set the tone for the session and lets the participants know that what will follow is not a typical "class." An icebreaker helps to build community among the participants—many of whom may not know each other—and a sense of trust that will come in handy as they are asked to share personal responses to discussion questions related to the theme. While a particular icebreaker is included with each session plan in Part I, they are interchangeable for most sessions. When a group is first meeting, it's wise to use an icebreaker that allows the participants to learn each other's names (for example, see page 117).

Teaching (about 15 minutes) The teaching covers some information about the main theme of the session as related to the particular month. It should be presented in an interesting and engaging manner. The teaching sections in Part I are not meant to be read out loud. Rather, put the teaching into your own words. Add your own personal anecdotes or stories related to the teaching as well as any interesting information you are able to dig up from other sources on the subject. Junior high age students are enamored with cultural and historical facts and trivia. When presented in an interesting way, your presentation of the teaching, though brief, can be information these participants will never forget and could lead them to further exploration of this topic important to Catholic tradition.

For each teaching, three "Additional Lessons" are listed. Some of these ideas offer scripture references or church teachings related to the main teaching. Others simply present related information that can be researched and expanded on when doing the teaching.

The approach for presenting the teaching is very simple. You can either sit on the open side of the semicircle or walk back and forth over the open space as you talk. After the sessions are up and running for a few months, you might want to choose other engaging adults or high school teens to handle the teaching part, as long as they are well-versed in the material and style of the presentation.

Discussion Questions (about 15 minutes) The participants should have a chance to respond to the teaching presentation. Normally, this is done by sharing responses to discussion questions related to the teaching.

Everyone should have the opportunity to share a response to a question. However, make sure to tell the participants that they can always "pass" if they would prefer not to answer a particular question. If the group is large, the participants may share their response with one person on either side of them. After allowing time for this, call on volunteers to share either their own response or the response of their partner with the entire group.

The responses may also be shared in small groups of three to five participants. If you choose this option, you need to have a quick way to divide the participants into small groups. One of the fastest ways is to break down by birthday months. For example, if you want to form four small groups, say, "All the people born in autumn sit in this corner of the room, all the people born in spring over here," etc. After the groups have formed, adjust for equal sizing and to separate kids who are more likely to cause trouble together.

It's helpful to assign leaders to each small group. High school teens work very well for this. They can get the group organized, begin the sharing, and make sure that everyone is heard. If you don't have group leaders, assign a person in each group as the designated first speaker by saying something like, "The person with the birthday nearest to today talks first."

Do the questions one at a time. Take them in order from easier to more difficult topics. They have already been arranged this way. Simply ask a question and have the participants respond in the method you have decided. Allow about five minutes for each question. Give a thirty-second warning before ending each question's discussion time.

Save a few minutes after discussion of the third question to call on volunteers to summarize what has been said for the entire group.

Project Ideas (about 25 minutes) The project portion of the session provides another way for the participants to apply the teaching. It is generally a hands-on individual assignment like a simple art project or a letter writing campaign. Some of the ideas involve service work for the parish or local community. Often, a portion of a video is recommended for viewing or a guest speaker is suggested to expand on the teaching.

Two project ideas are offered for each session. Sometimes you will have time for both projects, other times only one. Make sure to read the project ideas carefully so that you are aware of any materials you will need to bring or preparations you will need to make before the session.

Allow at least five minutes at the end of the project time to clean up materials, get the room back in order, and prepare for lunch.

The sessions included in Part I are arranged by month. Generally, the main themes can be covered on any Sunday in the month in which it is listed. When themes overlap months, two months are listed in which the session may be held.

Doing Lunch

Sharing a meal together is an important part of the Sunday event. The gradual uneasiness that begins dissipating among the junior highers at Mass, in the icebreaker exercise, and through the discussion and project times leads naturally to an informal and fun occasion for eating lunch.

Lunch can be planned to last up to a half an hour, but can be slightly shorter depending on the nature of the activity. Sometimes lunch is incorporated into the activity; for example, if the activity is a beach picnic, you don't have to have lunch first at the church and then lunch again on the picnic!

Once in a while, the church or a particular ministry may be able to kick in some funds to pay for the kids' lunches, but this isn't always necessary. If you do have some money to budget for these events, consider paying for the napkins, utensils, and condiments you might need.

Here are some of the easiest but nevertheless effective ways to handle lunches:

- Buy some cold cuts, chips, sodas, and cookies. Arrange the food cafeteria-style on a long counter or table. Have the participants move down the line and make their own sandwiches and fill their plates. When you advertise for the event, include the cost for lunch in the total price that the participants must pay.

- Using the same "hands-on" procedure, have a barbecue with hamburgers or hot dogs. Again, charge the participants a nominal fee.

- Have the teens bring their own sack lunches. This method is recommended when the group will soon be on the move.

- Build in some extra time to go to a nearby fast-food restaurant. This is a BYOF ("buy your own food") event.

- Send out for some pizzas.

If your Sunday event begins in the early morning or is held on a Saturday or Sunday evening, don't eliminate the meal; just change it to breakfast (donuts are the natural choice) or dinner (see pizza idea above).

Sunday Activities

From the kids' angle, the Sunday activities are the best part of the whole day. The more the activity appeals to a junior high kid's sense of fun, the more participants you will have at your event.

There are two important things to note as you begin to consider Sunday activities for the various months: 1) Many of the activities will cost the teens some money, and 2) You will need some other adults to help with chaperoning and transportation.

As to cost, be sure to give a "high" per person estimate for the event. For example, if the group is going to the movies, include the price of the ticket and a couple of extra dollars for snacks. Arrange parent chaperones and transportation well in advance of the event, possibly at the beginning of the program year.

Also, make sure you arrange for the proper legal permissions you will need from the parents or guardians of the participants. You should have signed forms that not only grant permission for participation but also record medical information and authorization concerning each person. The school principal or parish DRE is bound to have a supply of these types of forms.

There is some method to the madness of planning the activities. For instance, you usually wouldn't want to schedule a snow sledding activity for August or a swim party for January. Also, while the really big events like trips to an amusement park will attract lots of kids, it's better not to do two of these in a row. For the event following a Six Flags trip, try something simpler like an afternoon of softball or gym games. Generally, the events should not last more than three hours. Parents appreciate having their sons and daughters home at an early hour on a Sunday evening, with Monday morning right around the corner. If you are planning an event that works better in the evening (like a dance), it's better to hold it on a Saturday than a Sunday.

Thirty-six Sunday activities—nine activities for each of the four seasons: winter, spring, summer, and fall—are offered in Part II. Each activity lists the basic preparations that will need to be made and a description of the activity itself. Feel free to arrange and adapt the activities to your local climate and to the group's interests.

Other Positive Aspects of the Program

Sponsoring a once-a-month Sunday event that includes Mass, a teaching session, lunch, and an activity has many obvious benefits, but there are many other underlying benefits as well, including:

No registration or attendance is required. A person can come one month and skip the next. Though you don't take "official" attendance, it's wise to work with other adult and high school teen leaders to introduce yourself to all the participants and take their names so that you will be able to refer them to other programming in the parish.

The cost is minimal. Generally, the participants pay for their lunch and any fees associated with an activity.

The events offer a chance for large group evangelization. Many junior highers on the parish rolls who have not participated in any religious programming in years will return for a Sunday event. Also, the junior high participants can and do invite many of their "unchurched" friends to these events. Remember, Mass is the ticket in. Many of the non-Catholic friends are able to provoke interesting questions and discussion related to their Mass and session attendance.

High school teens make great volunteers. Forget the latest NBA star; it's the high school teens who are the junior high kids' heroes. Many high school teens are looking for service opportunities in their parish or community. Most who sign on as volunteers for these events are happy they did. High school teens can be used to conduct icebreakers, lead teaching presentations, moderate small group discussions, help with projects and lunch, and chaperone the activities.

Your parish has a separate junior high youth ministry. Go ahead and count it as such. Some youth ministries make the mistake of involving junior high age kids in the high school youth ministry program. This is usually a big mistake, as the older teens will eventually stop coming as the program becomes inundated with the younger ones. (By the way, it's your call if you want to invite sixth graders to participate with seventh and eighth graders. If sixth graders do not attend the same school as the seventh and eighth graders, you should probably not include them in this program.)

It's Catholic through and through. Not only does the Sunday event include mandatory Mass attendance, but the teachings are based heavily on the structure of the liturgical year and the calendar of the saints' feasts. Participants learn about Catholic practices, traditions, and saints that may have escaped them even in regular curriculums.

Religious education students and Catholic school students come together. This is a worthy goal as you begin to unite all the teens and pre-teens of your parish in what you hope will be an expanding youth ministry through the high school years.

The rest of the book provides the foundation for getting the Sunday event program up and running.

Part I

Sunday Sessions
Month-by-Month

Mary, the Mother of God

Session Topics: Mary, living God's will, vocation, Nestorianism, heresy

Icebreaker

Divide the group into two teams on opposite sides of the room. The object of the game is to see how fast each team can ready one of its members for school. You will need a stopwatch or watch with a second hand. Provide the following items for each team: (1) a large button-down shirt, (2) a baseball hat, (3) an individual size box of cereal, (4) a small carton of milk, (5) a spoon and bowl, (6) a toothbrush and toothpaste, (7) a book bag, and (8) several books and/or notebooks scattered around the playing area. Ask each team to choose one player to be the representative student. Tell them the object of the game is to assist their representative in getting ready for school before the alarm clock goes off. (For example, team members can prepare the cereal and milk and help locate the supplies for the book bag.) Set the alarm for five minutes. Choose one team to go first. Keep exact time of how long it takes for the representative to (1) put on the shirt and button every button, (2) eat the entire bowl of cereal, (3) brush his or her teeth, (4) gather all the books into the book bag, and (5) put on the baseball hat backward. After the first team has finished, call on the other. The team that prepares its representative the fastest wins.

Teaching

A few years ago a new specialty gift hit the market around Christmas time. What looked like a clock actually didn't keep time in the traditional way. Rather, what you were supposed to do was enter your age (in years, months, and days), your gender, and the area of the world where you lived. Turned on, the "clock" then programmed your life expectancy (for example, seventy-seven years, eight months, and two days) and began a systematic countdown in minutes to zero, the end of your life.

Would *you* like a product that told you that you have only 32,587,200 minutes left to live?

Really, our lives are not so certain and can't be calculated accurately that way. Though we can and should plan for tomorrow, none of us is absolutely sure of what tomorrow will bring. We never really know what to expect.

Mary must have lived like that. She was a very young person—maybe about your age—when she gave birth to Jesus. The events of the preceding months must have seemed like a whirlwind to her: first an engagement, then a surprise pregnancy with the news that her child would be God's chosen one, then childbirth in a strange place miles away from her own village.

After the shepherds visited there, they went out and told everyone that this young girl's child was the Messiah and the Lord.

As the scriptures tell us, "Mary kept all these things, reflecting on them in her heart" (Lk 2:19). New Year's Day is a holy day dedicated to Mary, the Mother of God.

Many years ago, a fifth-century bishop named Nestorius claimed that there were two persons in Christ—one divine, the other human. Along with this heresy, or false teaching, Nestorius said that Mary was the mother of only the human person Jesus, not the mother of the divine person. A church council at Chalcedon clarified what the church believed: *Jesus is one person with two natures, human and divine. And, Mary is truly the Mother of God.*

What a dramatic turn life took for the young Jewish girl from Nazareth. In accepting what God wanted of her, Mary received the most esteemed title any human being could hope to attain: Mother of God.

As you begin this new year, what surprises does God have in store for you? And, if you are presented with a challenge, will you accept it or wallow in fear at the thought of trying something new? Be open to possibilities as Mary was. Life rarely flows in a completely orderly fashion from junior high, to high school, to college, to marriage, to career, to retirement, to death without some zigzagging along the way. Take time to reflect on the events in your life with all your heart. Do more than simply count down the days and minutes. Live your life for today as God intends.

Additional Lessons

 Examine three occasions in the scriptures where Mary reflected on the events taking place in her life and the life of her son: Luke 2:19, 2:33, and 2:51. Lead a silent reflection where the participants can meditate on the events of their day and week.

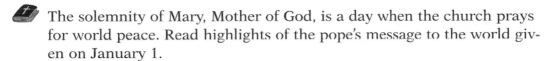 The solemnity of Mary, Mother of God, is a day when the church prays for world peace. Read highlights of the pope's message to the world given on January 1.

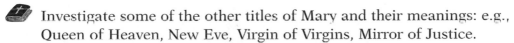 Investigate some of the other titles of Mary and their meanings: e.g., Queen of Heaven, New Eve, Virgin of Virgins, Mirror of Justice.

Discussion Questions

1. What is one devotion you or someone you know practices to honor Mary?
2. If someone could tell you the exact day and hour you will die, would you want to know? How would you live your life differently if you knew when you were going to die?
3. Life often zigzags away from the plans we have made for ourselves. Tell about a time that something unexpected happened to you and how you handled it.

Project Ideas

Have each person write five New Year's resolutions in prayer form on small slips of paper. For example, "Dear God, I promise to pray more often," or, "Lord, I promise to stop teasing the seventh grader with the locker near mine." Give each person a letter size envelope and a stamp. Tell them to seal their resolutions in the envelope and address it to themselves. At the end of the year they can note the date of the postmark, break the seal, and reread their resolutions to see how they did.

Pass out a fine-tip marker and a 3" x 5" index card to each person. Have them neatly print a traditional Marian prayer (see below) that they can keep near their beds. Practice the prayer with the teens until they have memorized it.

Memorare

Remember, O most gracious Virgin Mary,
that never was it known
that anyone who fled to thy protection,
implored thy help, or sought thy intercession
was left unaided.
Inspired by this confidence,
I fly unto thee, O Virgin of virgins, my Mother;
to thee I come,
before thee I stand, sinful and sorrowful.
O Mother of the Word Incarnate,
despise not my petitions,
but in thy mercy hear and answer me.
Amen.

The Baptism of Jesus

Session Topics: baptism of Jesus, parent/child relationships, vocation

Icebreaker

Divide the group into two teams. Have each person write on a piece of paper three facts about himself or herself that not many would know. For example, "I was born in Yakima, Washington," or, "My grandmother was an extra in *The Sound of Music*." Have them sign their names at the bottom of the papers. Collect the papers in two piles, keeping each team's separate. Choose a paper from one team and read one of the facts. Allow the members of the other team to confer and see if they can guess who wrote it. If they are correct, award three points. If not, read another fact and allow another guess. A correct answer for this round is worth two points. Continue with a third fact, if necessary, and award one point for a correct answer. If the team fails to give a correct answer, they get no points. Then choose another paper from the other pile, read the facts one at a time, and solicit guesses from the other team. Play for a few rounds. Then have everyone pair up with a partner (on either team), introduce himself or herself, and tell one fact about his or her life. If there is time, call on each person to introduce his or her partner to the entire group.

Teaching

God the Father had special plans for his Son.

Jesus was anointed, or specially chosen, by God his Father to "bring light and God's promise of hope" to everyone.

What have you been specially chosen to be or do?

Your parents have dreams for you. They probably hope you will go to college, prepare for a career, and then work at a job you like. Also, they likely hope that

25

some day you will be able to marry and have a family. Most of all, your parents hope you will continue to practice your Catholic faith and deepen your relationship with God.

These big dreams are pretty basic to most people who have children. Sometimes you might feel cramped by the expectations your parents have for you or bothered by the pressure they seem to put on you. Maybe you have a dad who seems discouraged when you don't get to play as much as the other kids on a team and critiques your every move when you do play. Or, maybe your mom constantly nags you about your grades, even though you have mostly Bs. Both parents may put strict curfews on your after-school activities and severely judge some of your peers. What should you make of this?

First, your parents are not perfect. Nobody gave them a class on how to parent teenagers. They are doing the best they can, but they are bound to make some mistakes. Cut them some slack.

Second, your parents love you. If you've ever cared for a younger sibling or baby-sat any small child, you can kind of understand how easy it is to be protective of someone. Your parents have been your age. They know about the consequences associated with the choices you make. Likely, their only agenda is that they hope to guide you to make the right choices for yourself.

When Jesus was anointed at his baptism, the sky opened, and his Father's voice could be heard: "You are my own dear Son, and I am pleased with you." Even if you haven't heard it for a while, imagine your own parents saying similar words to you. And know the same God who loved Jesus also loves you.

Additional Lessons

God's servant is called to bring justice to all the nations (Is 42:4). Define justice as "fairness" or "righteousness" for all.

Read or recount one of the gospel accounts of Jesus' baptism: Matthew 3:13-17, Mark 1:9-11 or Luke 3:21-22.

Teach a brief lesson on the Trinity. Point out that all three persons of the Trinity are present at Jesus' baptism.

Discussion Questions

1. What is one expectation your parents have for you? Is this mostly a fair expectation? Why?
2. Imagine it is the end of your life. You look back on all your years and realize that there was one accomplishment that stood out above all the rest. What is this accomplishment?
3. John the Baptist was a humble friend of the Lord, saying he was "not good enough to even untie his sandals." Of course, Jesus' ministry was based in humble service of others. What does humility mean to you? When was a time you did something humbly?

Project Ideas

Have each person prepare an individual time capsule to be opened on the date of his or her high school graduation. The "capsule" can be an empty two-liter soda bottle. Have the students fill out papers telling about their likes and dislikes now (e.g., favorite music, book, movie, best friend, etc.) and their goals and dreams for their years in high school. Give each person a piece of masking tape. Have them print: "Not to be opened until June 20 __ __."

Give each person two popsicle sticks and two 18" pieces of yarn (two different colors). Have them glue the sticks to form a cross and wrap the yarn around the middle to form a creative design.

Martin Luther King, Jr.

Session Topics: Martin Luther King, Jr., racism and catholicity, beatitude

Icebreaker

Divide the participants into small groups of five or six. Give each person a baseball card. (The baseball cards should all be the same brand and the same year and have as much detailed statistics and information about the players as possible.) Explain how to read the back of the cards as needed. Ask questions pertaining to the cards, for example, "What was the most home runs hit in one season by your player?" Tell the participants to share the answer with their group. Tell each group to choose the highest answer and share with everyone. Award one point to the team with the player who hit the most home runs in one season. Play a few rounds using other questions. For example:

- Which group has the most pitchers?
- Which group has the most National League players?
- Which group has the most players born in California?
- Which group has the most players born after 1975?
- Which group has the most left-handers?
- Which group has the player with the most RBIs?

Play a predetermined number of rounds or points.

Teaching

Branch Rickey, the managing partner of the Brooklyn Dodgers, was the man who signed Jackie Robinson as the first black man to play baseball in the all-white major leagues in 1947.

29

But the story began much earlier. In April of 1904 Rickey was a twenty-one-year-old coach of Ohio Wesleyan University, a Christian school. He took his team to South Bend, Indiana, to play Notre Dame. Checking into a hotel, the clerk refused to give a room to the team's only black player, Charles Thomas. Rickey told the clerk to set up a cot in his room. Thomas would stay with him.

Shortly after, Rickey called a team meeting.

"I tried to talk, but I couldn't take my eyes off Tommy," Rickey later recounted. "Here was this fine young man, sitting on the edge of his chair, crying. He was crying as though his heart would break.

"He was pulling frantically at his hands, and started muttering, 'Black skin. Black skin. If I could only make them white.

"'It's my skin, Mr. Rickey. If I could just tear it off, I'd be like everyone else.'"

Martin Luther King, Jr., the great civil rights activist whose birthday is commemorated with a holiday on January 15, would understand the pain Charles Thomas endured. In his famous "I Have a Dream" speech, King said that black people were "still languishing in the corners of American society" and were "exiles in their own land."

If you are a Catholic you can't be a racist. In fact the terms are completely contradictory. The definition of a racist is someone who excludes others on the basis of their race. Oppositely, "catholic" means "universal, open to all." The church takes pride in its diversity of races and cultures and its charge to spread the good news to all corners of the earth.

Jesus understood the pain of racism. He preached and gathered to himself the outcasts of society. He called these the *anawim*, or poor in spirit. In his famous Sermon on the Mount, Jesus said: "Blessed are the poor in spirit, for theirs is the kingdom of heaven" (Mt 5:3).

Make a pledge to be open to others, not exclusionary. Follow the examples of Branch Rickey and Martin Luther King, Jr., not the hotel clerk in South Bend who wouldn't give a man a bed only because of the color of his skin. Follow the example of Jesus who gathered the poor in spirit around him and called them blessed. He told them: "Blessed are you when they insult you and persecute you and utter every kind of evil against you because of me. Rejoice and be glad, for your reward will be great in heaven" (Mt 5:11-12).

Additional Lessons

 The relationship between Jews and Samaritans approximates contemporary examples of racism. Many of the people of Samaria (a region in central Palestine) were Jews who had intermarried with Gentiles during the Assyrian captivity. During Jesus' time, Jews bypassed the region altogether as they traveled between Galilee and Judea. Cite gospel examples that refer to this strained relationship: Luke 9:52-54, 10:25-37, 17:11-19, and John 8:48. Then read examples of Jesus' response to this behavior: his healing of a Samaritan leper (Lk 17:11-19), the conversation with the Samaritan woman at the well (Jn 4:4-42), and the telling of the parable of the good Samaritan (Lk 10:30-37).

Using a biography of Martin Luther King, Jr., list and briefly explain the highlights of the civil rights movement that spanned his life.

The *anawim* described in the beatitudes were those without material possessions who depended completely on God for everything. Ask the participants to tell you about people they know or know of who fit the definition of *anawim* today.

Discussion Questions

1. Why do you think people from different races still have so much trouble getting along?
2. Tell about a time when you were excluded from an activity for no good reason or a time when you excluded someone else.
3. How do you respond when someone you are with makes a racist statement?

Project Ideas

Ask an older parishioner who grew up in a time marked by racism to give a short group presentation detailing society's (and his or her own) changing attitudes during the course of his or her life.

In small groups have the participants role-play peaceful resolutions to situations that are often marked by racial tensions (for example: teens of different races sharing the same lunch room, a teen's parents reacting to a son/daughter dating someone of a different race, two schools with students of different races competing in an athletic contest).

The Presentation of the Lord

Session Topics: presentation of Jesus, salvation for all of humankind

Icebreaker

Collect Christmas trees and Christmas wreaths that still need to be discarded. Have the participants help to dig a large outdoor bonfire pit. Have a bonfire burning the trees and wreaths. Sing "O Come All Ye Faithful" as one last tribute to the Christmas season.

Teaching

According to ancient Jewish law, a woman who gave birth to a boy was unable to touch anything sacred or enter the Temple area until forty days after the birth of her son. This period of purification was observed by Mary. The law also prescribed that after the forty days the mother should offer a year-old lamb as a sin offering, or if she were poor, two turtledoves or two young pigeons. According to the gospel, this ritual was also followed by Joseph and Mary, who presented their son for purification at the Temple in Jerusalem.

While there, Jesus' parents met a man named Simeon whom the gospel describes as "righteous and devout" and as someone who was awaiting the time when salvation would come to God's people in Israel. When Simeon saw the infant Jesus he took him into his arms and said:

"Now, Master, you may let your servant go
    in peace, according to your word,
for my eyes have seen your salvation,
    which you prepared in sight of all the peoples,
a light for revelation to the Gentiles,
    and glory for your people Israel" (Lk 2:29-32).

The feast of the Presentation of the Lord is traditionally celebrated in the church on February 2, forty days after Christmas. In many places the day marks the end of the Christmas season. Christmas decorations are taken down and Christmas trees and plants are burned and mixed with the remaining ashes of the Yule log. These ashes are then spread over gardens and fields in hopes of a bountiful spring crop.

From Simeon's words that Jesus would not only be the source of salvation for Jews, but "a light of revelation to the Gentiles," the day also is called Candlemas. Sometimes blessed candles are handed out to celebrate the feast. In Latin America, statues of the baby Jesus are decorated in fine infant clothing. Cakes are shared with the figure of the baby Jesus outlined in sugar.

What can we learn from the feast of the Presentation to deepen our own relationships with Jesus? First, we learn that his parents were pious Jews who followed religious laws. Second, they were poor, as they were unable to afford a year-old lamb for sacrifice. Also, we learn that many people waited in expectation for Jesus and that his birth was an open invitation to all people to share in the joy of salvation.

Additional Lessons

Research and present other names, traditions, and folklore associated with the feast of the Presentation of the Lord, both locally and from all over the world.

Read and share the laws from the Hebrew scriptures on the period of purification (Lv 12:2-8) and the presentation of a newborn (Ex 13:1-2).

Read Simeon's prophecy about Jesus' destiny (Lk 2:34-35). Discuss how this prophecy would eventually be fulfilled.

Discussion Questions

1. What is your earliest memory of being brought to church and attending Mass?
2. What is the most amazing thing someone (teacher, neighbor, relative) ever said to your parents about you?
3. What is something you hope to accomplish in your life that would bring you complete fulfillment as Simeon experienced when he held the infant Jesus?

Project Ideas

Give each person a lighted candle. Process with the candles to the church or chapel to a crib or manger display of the infant Jesus. Say a prayer and have a candle blessing. Then have the participants extinguish their candles and help to put away any Christmas decorations that remain in the church.

Cut a large tray of cake or brownies so that each person gets his or her own piece. Pass out a spoon with pinch of white sugar to each person. Have them design with sugar a sketch to represent Jesus (crib, cross, etc.) on the cake. Display all the pieces on one table. Then have everyone eat his or her piece in celebration of this feast.

St. Valentine's Day

Session Topics: Valentine's Day, infatuation, love, commitment

Icebreaker

Have a traditional "Sadie Hawkins race." Clear out one large open space in the center of the room. Have all the boys sit in the middle. Divide the girls in two equal groups on both sides of the boys. When you say "go" have the girls go to the center and carry the boys back to their side without dragging them on the ground. (It will take more than one girl to carry one boy.) Tell the boys that they must sit passively. They cannot resist and they cannot help. The team with the most boys on its side wins.

Teaching

February 14 is a greeting card holiday of "love" associated with a Christian saint, St. Valentine. How this connection was ever made is the subject of many questionable tales and lore.

First off, there are many St. Valentines and two are mentioned as being martyred, or killed for their faith, on this day. One Valentine died in Rome, the other about sixty miles from Rome at a place called Interamna. There is little evidence of either man's life, though tradition has it that the Roman Valentine was a priest who was persecuted by the emperor Claudius the Goth in about the year 269.

More interesting is how this day became a day of courtship and romance, eventually marked by exchanging of love notes or "Valentines." English literature mentions that around the "time of St. Valentine's day" birds began to pair, the first sign of spring.

Your school principal or teacher may be able to make similar observations about the behavior of boys and girls around the middle of February. One teacher tells this story:

> In September Hardy and Marcy were sworn enemies. In October Marcy told anyone who would listen that Hardy made her sick. Something happened just before Christmas. At a school dance, Hardy and Marcy were the best dancers in the school. A bond was formed. Now at Valentine's Day, all the kids in class are abuzz because Hardy and Marcy are 'going together,' whatever that means!

Valentine's Day is a good time of the year to take stock of your own friendships, your sexual feelings, and the true meaning of love. Many times teenagers confuse infatuation with love. Infatuation describes any kind of relationship that includes sexual attraction or sexual feelings. You can be infatuated with many different people, including people you don't know well or don't know at all. Infatuations come and go.

Love is different. Love is a feeling that is long-lasting. It involves other feelings like commitment, compassion, care, trust, respect, and sacrifice. You already know this because you have been loved and have loved others, especially your parents and other family members.

Romantic love combines the sexual feelings associated with infatuation with the deep and true commitment for another that can happen only after you really get to know a person well.

In any case, enjoy sending cards and notes to your special friends and people you care about on Valentine's Day. Just make sure the notes and messages you send and receive honestly express what you want to say and what you believe.

Finally, think about sending a card or note to someone you know who might not otherwise get a Valentine. Also, this is the perfect holiday to express your love for people you know who really do love you: your parents, grandparents, brothers and sisters.

Additional Lessons

Present a more detailed lesson on the church's teaching on sexuality and committed romantic love in the context of marriage in conjunction with the parents and established family life programs in your parish or diocese.

Discuss how of the virtues of faith, hope, and love, only love remains unto eternity. Read and share 1 Corinthians 13:1-13, the way of love.

Using a biography on the lives of the saints, present any other information or folklore on St. Valentine.

Discussion Questions

1. What is your favorite Valentine card you have ever received or given?
2. Infatuations come and go. Cite an example from your own life or the life of someone you know that supports this statement.
3. Why do you think true love always includes lasting commitment?

Project Ideas

Divide the participants into small groups of four or five. Have them write letters of affirmation to each person in their group, addressing them by name and affirming their talents and gifts.

Give each person a large heart cut-out from white construction paper. Ask them to write a love note to God in the center of the heart. They can sign it if they wish. Collect all the hearts and attach them to a large piece of red poster paper. Hang the poster in the meeting area.

February

The Beginning of Lent

Session Topics: Lent, Mardi Gras, Ash Wednesday, sacramentals, penance, Forty Hours Devotion

Icebreaker

Show part of the movie *Groundhog Day* with Bill Murray, in which Murray finds himself living the events of Groundhog Day over and over. Ask the participants to go around in a circle and tell one day they would like to live over if they could. If there is time, have them go around again and tell about one day they would not ever want to relive.

Teaching

Lent is an important season in the church year. Lent lasts for forty full days, not including the Sundays that fall in between Ash Wednesday and the conclusion of the Mass of the Lord's Supper on Holy Thursday night. The word *Lent* is taken from an English word that means "spring."

Lent is traditionally seen as a time of fasting and doing penance, in imitation of the fast that Jesus undertook for forty days prior to the beginning of his ministry (Lk 4:1-13).

In the early years of the church, the requirements for fasting were severe. For example, in the seventh century, Pope Saint Gregory wrote: "We abstain from flesh meat and from all things that come from flesh, such as milk, cheese, eggs—and butter of course."

During those times, as Ash Wednesday approached, families used up any of those food products that could not be eaten during Lent. From this practice have come such holidays as Mardi Gras (Fat Tuesday) and Carnival ("removal of meat"). Celebrations were and continue to be part of the pre-lenten week. The

Mardi Gras festival in New Orleans is held on the weekend preceding the Tuesday before Lent.

Partly due to all of the partying, in 1748 Pope Benedict XIV began a special "Forty Hours Devotion" for the three days before Lent to allow people to do penance and pray for any sins they may have committed during the Mardi Gras time. The Forty Hours Devotion is still practiced in Catholic parishes today. Usually it begins with the celebration of Mass. Then the Blessed Sacrament, a large host, is placed in a fancy container called a monstrance, carried through the church by a priest, and then placed on the altar where the parishioners can visit the real presence of Jesus for the next forty hours. The devotion ends with another Mass or a special eucharistic devotion called Benediction.

Today there are not as many official penance requirements during Lent. In the United States, Ash Wednesday and Good Friday are days of fasting (for anyone over the age of 21) and abstinence (for anyone over the age of 14). Fasting means that only one main meal and two smaller meals may be eaten. Abstinence means that no meat or meat products may be eaten on these days or on any Friday of Lent.

On Ash Wednesday, ashes burned from the palm leaves from the previous Palm Sunday are placed on the foreheads of Catholics in the sign of the cross, reminding them to do penance during Lent. At the same time, the minister says, "Remember, you are dust and unto dust you shall return." The wearing of ashes is a public display of our sinfulness, much in the same way that Israelite sinners from the Old Testament and early Christians known as public sinners wore sackcloth and ashes as public penances for their sins. The blessed ashes are also a *sacramental*. A sacramental is an object, prayer, or blessing that is known by Christians to be sacred in some way. For example, a rosary, the sign of the cross, and a crucifix are other examples of sacramentals.

Lent remains a time for doing penance, for "giving up" some food or area of enjoyment as a sign that you are sharing in the way of the cross that Jesus undertook leading up to his crucifixion. Such self-discipline can help you from becoming spiritually lazy.

Lent is also a time for doing something extra and worthwhile. You may make a promise to help an elderly neighbor with yard work or visit your grandparents more. And, you can make a greater effort to pray during Lent. Remember, Lent is a time of preparation so that you can enjoy more fully the great rewards of Jesus' resurrection on Easter Sunday.

Additional Lessons

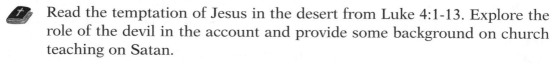 Read the temptation of Jesus in the desert from Luke 4:1-13. Explore the role of the devil in the account and provide some background on church teaching on Satan.

List and tell about several other sacramentals.

Explain the doctrine of real presence in the eucharist.

Discussion Questions

1. When you receive ashes on Ash Wednesday, do you leave them on all day or rub them off? Why?
2. What is something you will "give up" for penance during Lent? What is something you will do during Lent to bring yourself closer to Jesus?
3. Tell about a time when you were tempted to ignore God and follow Satan. What did you do?

Project Ideas

Take a tour of the sacristy and view the monstrance, as well as the other sacred vessels including the chalice. Ask a priest or other sacristan to explain their histories and significance.

If the session takes place before Lent, arrange for a Mardi Gras feast. Have the participants work together to make (and eat) homemade ice cream. Or, have them put their own toppings on ice cream sundaes.

Laetare Sunday

Session Topics: Laetare Sunday, joy, Lent, catechumenate, Apostles' Creed

Icebreaker

Ask how many have a good (clean) joke to share. Tell those who raise their hands to move off stage. Then tell the remaining participants they will rate the jokes by holding up their fingers and using a scale of 1 to 10 (10 being the funniest). Call on the comedians one at a time to tell their jokes. Award a prize to the winner based on the audience's ratings.

Teaching

Imagine yourself in a line-up prior to gym class. The teacher is really frightening, walking back and forth before everyone marking down the grades of those not wearing the right color socks or those not standing in their assigned place. The scene is very dismal. Then, suddenly, from in the back someone begins to giggle softly. The giggling increases to full-scale laughter among everyone in that area. Soon enough the entire class is bent over laughing hysterically. Then, surprise of surprise, even the mean gym teacher joins in. A dark and dreary time has been transformed to one of fun and joy.

There is a similar event that takes place right in the middle of Lent. On the fourth Sunday of Lent the previously dreary church sanctuary may be decorated with flowers, and more upbeat music may be played. The priest may wear rose-colored vestments instead of the purple penitential ones.

Why the change? This midpoint of Lent is known as Laetare Sunday. Laetare is a Latin word that means "rejoice." The reason for the rejoicing is that it is on this Sunday or shortly after that those preparing for baptism at the Easter vigil (the "catechumens") receive the sacred text of the Apostles' Creed for the first

45

time. Remember, a creed is a list of beliefs held as central by a group. The reception of the Creed by the catechumens signifies that the time of their full membership into the community of the church is near.

For this reason, the church can hardly contain its joy on Laetare Sunday. In previous centuries, as a symbol of this joy, the pope would carry a golden rose in his right hand when leaving Mass. Later, the golden rose consisted of a cluster of roses made of pure gold that the popes would bless and then give to cities, churches, or shrines as a memento.

In England, a tradition around Laetare Sunday had the boys and girls who lived away at school returning home to their "mother church" where they had been baptized, bringing with them gifts to place at the altar. Adult children would visit their own mothers on this day. For these reasons, Laetare Sunday also became known as "Mothering Sunday."

Soon after the catechumens receive the Creed, they also are given the text of the Our Father. These ceremonies are for those catechumens who have dutifully completed the long preparation process—today usually called the catechumenate or Rite of Christian Initiation of Adults—and have passed the tests and scrutinies of faith. You may have noticed catechumens at your parish who leave Mass immediately after the homily. They then go to another area outside of the church where they can do further study on the scripture readings and church doctrines. On the night of the Easter vigil, they will be welcomed into full communion with the church, receiving the sacraments of baptism, confirmation, and eucharist. Then they will be able to stay for the entire Mass. Laetare Sunday is celebrated in anticipation of that occasion.

Additional Lessons

Have the participants memorize the Apostles' Creed, and cover in more detail the meaning of each creedal statement.

Review the signs and rituals of baptism, confirmation, and eucharist as sacraments of initiation.

Explain these stages of the catechumenate: inquiry, catechumenate, enlightenment, and mystagogy.

Discussion Questions

1. When was a time when you experienced joy or happiness in an otherwise dreary or sad situation?
2. What is a creedal statement that you have a question about or trouble understanding?
3. If you could give the catechumens from your parish one piece of advice about belonging to your parish, what would it be?

Project Ideas

Have the participants write welcome notes to the catechumens that can be delivered to them after the Easter vigil.

If the session is held before Laetare Sunday, collect real flowers or spray artificial roses with gold paint. Have the participants on hand to give one or more flowers to the catechumens as they are dismissed from the liturgy.

St. Joseph's Day

Session Topics: St. Joseph, family history, genealogy, the announcement of Jesus' birth

Icebreaker

Display several photos of slightly older teenagers and young adults who once participated in youth programs at your parish and whom you know something about. Tell the current participants about these older teens: what they were like then, what they have accomplished in the years since, what you learned about life and faith from them, what legacy they have left the current group, etc. If possible, have one of the older teens speak to the group on these topics.

Teaching

Interestingly, in the genealogy of Jesus found in the opening of the gospel of Matthew (1:1-17), Jesus' lineage is traced from Abraham, the patriarch of the Jewish people, through the generations, including King David, all the way through *Joseph,* not Mary his natural mother.

This is interesting because Joseph was not Jesus' biological father. Rather, Jesus was conceived by the Holy Spirit and born to the Virgin Mary. Jesus is the only begotten son of God the Father.

Yet the tracing of Jesus' family tree through Joseph and not his mother tells us two things: First, Joseph was known to be of the line of King David, a crucial element to those Jews who were awaiting the Messiah called for in the Hebrew scriptures. Second, the gospel writer and the early Christian community held Joseph in great esteem as Jesus' adopted father. Jewish parents were known for accepting and treating adopted children exactly the same as natural children.

From the gospels, we do not know much else about the life of Joseph. From Matthew's gospel we find out that Joseph had decided to call off his marriage with Mary when he discovered she was pregnant. But an angel from the Lord came to Joseph in a dream and said, "Joseph, the baby that Mary will have is from the Holy Spirit. Go ahead and marry her. Then after her baby is born, name him Jesus, because he will save people from their sins" (based on Mt 1:20-21). Joseph wed Mary soon after.

It is hard for us not to admire Joseph. He was the steady worker, the carpenter. Most of us admire people who go about their jobs without bragging or drawing attention to themselves. Certainly Joseph taught Jesus his work ethic. Certainly Jesus was nurtured and grew in love in the family of which Joseph was the head.

Devotion to Joseph did not officially take off until the fifteenth century. At that time, finally, Pope Sixtus IV established an annual feast for St. Joseph on March 19. St. Teresa of Avila had a special devotion to Joseph and established nineteen convents under his patronage.

Devotions continued to spread worldwide. In Italy and in Italian parishes in the United States, St. Joseph's Day is widely commemorated with a "St. Joseph Table" filled with many fine foods. On the east coast of Spain, fires are burned in honor of St. Joseph, a custom that is said to have been started by carpenters who cleaned out their workshops in his honor on March 19.

Joseph knew Jesus longer and more intimately than anyone else, other than Mary. He was a model of humble yet strong discipleship. How are you attracted to his example? What are some ways you can imitate his devotion to the Lord?

Additional Lessons

Read and compare the annunciation to Joseph in Matthew 1:18-25 with the annunciation to Mary in Luke 1:26-38.

Point out a major difference in the genealogy of Jesus recorded in Matthew 1:1-17 with the one in Luke 3:23-38: in Luke's gospel, Jesus' family tree extends to Adam, not Abraham, as Luke emphasizes Jesus' inclusive mission to the Gentiles.

Trace the development of the feasts to St. Joseph, including mention of the feast of St. Joseph the Worker on May 1, established by Pope Pius XII in 1956.

Discussion Questions

1. Who is an adult besides one of your parents who is a model of faith for you? Explain.
2. Tell about the accomplishments of someone in your family history.
3. In your opinion, should adopted children be able to search out and contact their biological parents, even if those parents request confidentiality?

Project Ideas

Have the students sponsor a "St. Joseph Table" of cold cuts, vegetables, punch, and pastries for one or more segments of parishioners.

Have the students trace their own family histories. Ask them to pinpoint how and when their Catholic Christian faith first came to this country.

Institution of the Eucharist

Session Topics: eucharist, Holy Thursday, Mass of the Lord's Supper, Chrism Mass, humility, service, Triduum

Icebreaker

Have the group sit in a circle, and ask the participants to take off one shoe and put it in the center of the circle. Then randomly pass out a shoe to each person, making sure they don't get their own. Ask them to look closely at the shoes they hold and tell one positive thing about the shoe's owner based only on what they can tell from the shoe. If there is time, have them share a second positive comment.

Teaching

Holy Thursday commemorates Jesus' institution of the eucharist. It was at his last supper on this day that Jesus broke bread, gave it to his disciples, and said, "Take and eat; this is my body." He took the cup and said, "Drink from it, all of you."

The last supper meal was a traditional Passover meal held in a secret location in Jerusalem. The twelve apostles shared the meal with Jesus, including Judas who later betrayed him.

The gospels of Matthew, Mark, and Luke tell of the breaking of the bread and the sharing of the cup. In John's gospel, the institution of the eucharist is replaced with Jesus' washing of his disciples' feet (Jn 13:1-20). This is a model of service that Jesus expects his disciples to imitate after he is gone. It is also a pattern of the crucifixion that will follow, symbolizing the cleansing of sin from his death on the cross.

Both the sharing of the bread and wine and the washing of the feet are incorporated in the Mass of the Lord's Supper, held on Holy Thursday evening

This evening Mass is the only one of the day celebrated at parish churches. During the day, a Mass of the Chrism is celebrated in the main cathedrals of the diocese. (A cathedral is the church of the local bishop.) In the Mass of the Chrism, the local bishop blesses the holy oils (oils of the sick, holy chrism, and oils of the catechumens) that will be used in all of his parishes throughout the entire year.

The evening Mass of the Lord's Supper is one of the most impressive of the year. It marks the end of Lent and the beginning of the Triduum, the most sacred period of the church year that includes Good Friday, the Easter vigil, and Easter Sunday. Triduum is a Latin word that means "three days."

At the Mass of the Lord's Supper, the altar and vestments are a festive white. The Gloria, which has not been sung through Lent, returns along with the ringing of bells to begin the celebration. After the readings, the priest reconstructs Jesus' command to his disciples—to show love for one another by the washing of feet—by washing the feet of several parishioners. Holy Thursday is also called "Maundy Thursday," a name that comes from the Latin *mandatum*, which means command.

At the end of Mass, the altar is stripped bare by the priest, now wearing purple, symbolizing the body of Christ that was stripped of its garments. The Blessed Sacrament is carried in a procession, which often includes all of the congregation, to a side altar or other place of "repose" where people can come to keep company with the Lord, usually until midnight, just as the first disciples once waited with him in the garden of Gethsemane on the night before he died. In earlier times, it was a custom to visit seven altars of repose through the night. In Mexico, for example, these altars were finely decorated to serve as a throne for a large monstrance containing the host.

The people leave in silence following some time in prayer before the Blessed Sacrament.

Additional Lessons

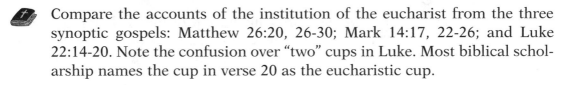 Compare the accounts of the institution of the eucharist from the three synoptic gospels: Matthew 26:20, 26-30; Mark 14:17, 22-26; and Luke 22:14-20. Note the confusion over "two" cups in Luke. Most biblical scholarship names the cup in verse 20 as the eucharistic cup.

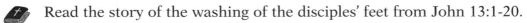 Read the story of the washing of the disciples' feet from John 13:1-20.

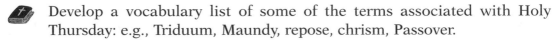 Develop a vocabulary list of some of the terms associated with Holy Thursday: e.g., Triduum, Maundy, repose, chrism, Passover.

Discussion Questions

1. Tell about at least one memory you have from attending the Mass of the Lord's Supper on Holy Thursday evening.

2. Jesus' washing of his disciples' feet was a model of humble service. What is one way you follow the example of humble service in your relationships with family, friends, or classmates?

3. What would it be like if you knew you were going to die tomorrow? How would you spend your final night?

Project Ideas

Ask the pastor to show the students the oils for the sick, the chrism, and the oils of the catechumens and to explain something of the composition of each.

Have the participants decorate paper bags with the names of those in the parish who have died in the past year. Next, have them make luminarias, setting votive candles in sand in the bags. The luminarias can be used to light an outdoor procession after the Holy Thursday Mass to the altar of repose.

Good Friday

Session Topics: Good Friday, service, death, sacrifice, redemption

Icebreaker

Make three different kinds of popcorn in three different bowls: one with butter and salt, one with salt only, and one with neither butter nor salt. Divide the participants into four equal groups. Have three groups sample and describe one kind of popcorn. Have the group with no popcorn tell what it feels like to have none. Relate the discussion to Jesus' life and the life of a disciple, to gradually give up everything in order to do God's will.

Teaching

One of the most commonly asked questions by children as they grow in their faith is, "Why do they call Good Friday *good* if that is the day that Jesus died?" You may have wondered about this yourself.

The answer is easily found in the Good Friday service. After the reading of the passion story from the gospel of John and the prayer intentions for the needs of the entire world, the priest processes with the crucifix down the center aisle, stopping three times and saying these words: "Behold the wood of the cross on which is hung our salvation."

This day that is outwardly dark and dismal actually commemorates Christ's greatest gift to us: though innocent, he was willing to accept death so that we might be saved from the power of Satan and sin. Good Friday is good because it opens the possibility that we might live forever.

Good Friday is the day that Christ died on the cross for the redemption of the world. Redemption is the act of recovering something that once was lost. When Adam and Eve sinned, humankind was plunged into sinfulness and lost the chance for eternity. Jesus' death redeemed us from sin. On Good Friday, the church does not celebrate Mass, the repetition of Christ's sacrifice on the cross. This is the only day of the year that this is true.

Rather, a service is offered in three parts: the scripture reading and prayer, the adoration of the cross, and the reception of communion. After the procession with the crucifix, the congregation likewise processes forward and venerates or honors the crucifix by kissing the feet of Jesus or reverently bowing before it. For communion, the consecrated bread that has been kept since the Holy Thursday Mass of the Lord's Supper at the altar of repose is retrieved and used.

After the service, the altar is stripped again, the tabernacle is left open, the sanctuary lights are snuffed out, and only the crucifix takes the place of honor in the center of the sanctuary. The congregation leaves the church in silence.

Over the years many other popular devotions and observances on Good Friday have developed. According to church law, Good Friday is a day of fasting and abstinence. In Ireland, many people hold what is called a "black fast," taking only water or tea on that day. Your family may have its own practices, for example, refraining from watching television or listening to music or doing any hard labor. Christians who go to public school often request an exemption from school on Good Friday for religious reasons. In parts of the Middle East, Christians replace their traditional daily greeting of *Shalom* ("Peace be with you") because these were the words Judas Iscariot used to betray Jesus. Instead, on Good Friday, they greet each other with "the light of God be with your departed ones."

Additional Lessons

Cover the doctrine of original sin (see the *Catechism of the Catholic Church*, 385-390).

Provide a brief background on the stations of the cross devotion.

Read the passion narrative from John 18:1-19:42.

Discussion Questions

1. What are some Good Friday customs or traditions you practice with your family?
2. How do you imagine the experience of death? What do you think happens to you after you die?
3. Tell about someone you know or know of who, though innocent, took the blame for another.

Project Ideas

Choose small groups of participants to act out the various stations of the cross. When prepared, pray the "living stations" with the entire group.

Take a collection of canned and packaged foods. Donate the collection to a soup kitchen or other agency for the poor. Arrange for the participants to tour the facility or hear a presentation from its representative as part of the project.

March / April

Easter Season

Session Topics: Easter, faith, hope, new life

Icebreaker

Invite a teen's mom or dad to participate in the first part of the session. The teen should not know that the parent is going to be there. When all have arrived, send the person whose parent will participate out of sight and sound from the group. Then invite the parent to speak briefly with the group and tell them one interesting (not embarrassing) fact about his or her son or daughter. Then dismiss the parent secretly and tell the teen to come back into the room. Spend the next few minutes having the group convince the person that his or her parent spoke to the group and told them something interesting about him or her (don't reveal "what" just yet). Note the person's reaction. Then finally tell him or her the interesting fact. Connect the exercise to the gospel story of "doubting Thomas."

Teaching

Easter is not a one-day holiday. In fact, it lasts for fifty days, beginning with the Easter vigil and lasting to the feast of Pentecost. (*Pentecost* comes from a Greek word that means "fiftieth day.")

In the liturgical year, the same gospel reading is heard on the second Sunday of Easter in all of the three reading cycles. The reading is from John 20:19-29 and is commonly referred to as the story of doubting Thomas. The reading gives us several clues to the early church's reaction to and understanding of the risen Jesus.

First, Jesus appears to the disciples "when the doors were locked," hinting at a body that was not made of flesh and bone. Jesus greets the disciples with "Peace be with you," reminding them of his words at the last supper when he said, "peace is my gift to you." When Jesus showed them his hands and his side, the disciples recognized him and were joyful. Then he breathed on them and said, "Receive the Holy Spirit." This recalls the second creation story from Genesis 2 where God brought life to Adam by breathing on him. Now, Jesus brings life in the Spirit to the disciples by breathing on them.

One of the disciples, Thomas, was not present during this appearance by Jesus. If you recall the story of Jesus' raising of his friend Lazarus, Thomas was the one who was afraid to return to Bethany, a small village near Jerusalem, in fear that the Jews would harm Jesus and him. When Jesus said, "Let us go to Lazarus," Thomas added: "Let us also go to die with him." It is easy to notice the skepticism in his voice.

Sometime after the risen Jesus' appearance, Thomas returns and utters his famous words: "Unless I see the mark of the nails in his hands and put my finger into the nail marks and put my hand into his side, I will not believe."

A week later Jesus returns and allows Thomas to do just as he requested. Jesus tells him: "Do not be unbelieving, but believe." Thomas then declares Jesus "My Lord and my God!" He is the first disciple to utter these words.

When you've heard this reading on the Sunday after Easter you may have felt that it was intended just for you and that you have even more esteem as a disciple of Jesus living two thousand years after he walked the earth. After all, you believe in the risen Jesus without ever having seen him, something that even St. Thomas, the doubting apostle, first failed to do.

Keep in mind the words Jesus said to Thomas: "Have you come to believe because you have seen me? Blessed are those who have not seen and have believed."

Additional Lessons

Uncover more of the life and legend of St. Thomas, including his missionary role in India.

Read and share biblical commentary on the other resurrection appearances of Jesus recorded in John 21.

Read St. Paul's answer to the questions "How are the dead raised?" and "With what kind of body will they come back?" from 1 Corinthians 15:36-49.

Discussion Questions

1. What will it take for you to *really* believe that Jesus is risen from the dead?
2. What do you think your body will be like after you die?
3. The church believes the risen Jesus is present in the world today. What are some concrete examples of his presence?

Project Ideas

Have the participants work in small groups to prepare a pantomime of John 20:19-29. The characters should act out the scene in silence as a narrator reads the passage.

Replicate a tradition from the island of Malta in which the men run as fast as they can, carrying a statue of Jesus to the top of a hill, indicating the motion of rising.

St. Mark

Session Topics: St. Mark, feast days, evangelists, synoptic gospels, discipleship

Icebreaker

Play a game like the old television program "I've Got A Secret." Print several categories on the board or a piece of newsprint: for example, family, friends, vacation, schoolwork, activities. Then call on one person to whisper a secret to you that no one else in the group will know for one of the areas: for example, "My great-grandfather was once mayor of our town." Tell the group the category (e.g., family). Allow them to ask up to ten yes-or-no questions prior to making a guess. The person who is able to correctly guess can be the next person to share a secret.

Teaching

April 25 is the feast day of St. Mark, the evangelist. A church *feast* commemorates a saint, an historical event, or some important theological concept. The feast days of saints began when communities of local Christians began to honor the death of a martyr by his or her grave. The early Roman calendar was a listing of all the martyrs who were honored in this way.

Evangelist is the name given to any one of the authors of the four gospel books. Mark is the name associated with the shortest of the gospels. Biblical scholarship also tells us that Mark's gospel was the first written, probably around 65 to 70 A.D., after the death of St. Peter. Many stories from Mark's gospel are also included in Matthew and Luke. For that reason these gospels are called the *synoptic* gospels, meaning "seen together."

Mark's gospel is concerned with telling who Jesus is and what his mission is. It is also concerned with defining what it means to be a disciple. *Disciple* is a word that means "learner." In the very first chapter and verse of his gospel, Mark discloses that Jesus is the "Christ, the Son of God." As we read on we find that, as readers, we have been given very privileged information, for in fact the disciples written about in the story—including Jesus' closest friend, Simon Peter—have no real knowledge of Jesus' identity. Many misunderstandings occur. When Peter misunderstands Jesus' mission to be one of great worldly power, Jesus calls him "Satan" and tells him: "You are thinking not as God does, but as human beings do" (Mk 8:33).

In fact, these misunderstandings are a part of a general theme known as the "messianic secret." For most of the gospel, only we as readers of the first verse, Jesus, and the demons are able to identify his purpose. Finally, in Mark 10:45, the pinnacle of the gospel, Jesus clearly defines who he is and what he is meant to accomplish: the Son of Man has come to serve and to give his life for all.

There is no clear biographical information about the author, Mark. It is assumed that he was a friend of Peter, and many early church leaders verified this. Peter himself referred to "my son Mark" (1 Pt 5:13) as being with him when he was in Rome.

A traditional story has been passed on that Mark included himself in the gospel. Since he would have been a young man at the time Jesus lived on earth, there is some feeling that Mark was the young man who followed Jesus after he had been arrested and all the other disciples had fled. According to the gospel, this young man was seized "but he left the cloth behind and ran off naked" (Mk 14:52).

Mark's gospel is intended to be read from start to finish in one reading. It is a good gospel for you to begin with in any study of Jesus and his message.

Additional Lessons

Investigate other theories about the identity of the author of Mark, especially the traditional understanding that he is the "John Mark" of Acts 12:12 and 25.

Read the three predictions of Jesus' passion (Mk 8:31-33; 9:30-32; 10:32-34) and note how the disciples misunderstand Jesus' words each time

List and explain other major feast days throughout the calendar year.

Discussion Questions

1. What is one question you have about Jesus that has never been answered adequately for you?
2. What would it take for you to give up everything in your life to follow Jesus?
3. If you were going to write a biography or story about Jesus, what would be your first sentence?

Project Ideas

Mark's gospel does not include an infancy narrative. Have the participants work together in small groups to make a list of other differences in the synoptics.

Make a list of question cards with answers that can only be found in the gospel of Mark (or have the participants make the question cards themselves). Divide the group in two. Play a game pitting team against team. Give each person a bible. Award points to the first team to come up with the correct answer.

Month of Mary

Session Topics: Mary, First Saturday, votive Masses, rosary, Mother's Day

Icebreaker

Play a team juggling game just for fun. Have the participants form circles of about eight people each. Give each circle a soft cushiony ball. Tell them the object of the game is for them to throw the ball in a pattern so that everyone gets a turn. For example, the first person throws across the circle to the second person. The second person throws to a third person, etc. After everyone has received a throw once, the real juggling begins as the group throws again in the same pattern. As a follow-up, you may want to play one more round with all of the participants in one big circle.

Teaching

You may know that May is the month of Mary. It was once traditional in Catholic schools to have a "May crowning" where students spent one day collecting and weaving spring flowers into a crown for Mary. On the next day, a "May queen," usually an eighth grade girl, was chosen to carry the crown in a school-wide procession to a statue of Mary, either in church or out-of-doors. Then, the May queen would climb a ladder and gently place the crown on Mary's head as the rest of the student body sang a song to honor Mary.

Mary also has her own day dedicated to her in each and every week throughout the year. The tradition of honoring Mary on Saturday goes back to the very first Holy Saturday, the day that Jesus lay in the tomb. It was Mary who waited anxiously but faithfully on that day in anticipation of the resurrection.

At the Council of Trent in the sixteenth century, the practice of offering a special or "votive" Mass to Mary on Saturdays was included in the Roman Missal, the official text for Masses. The Second Vatican Council in the 1960s also supported this tradition.

Catholics are called to do something special to honor Mary on Saturdays, especially during the Saturdays of May. This may include attending a Saturday morning Mass, doing a special work of charity, or praying the rosary.

The rosary is a special prayer of fifteen decades of Hail Marys that form a mantra or background for meditating on key events from the life of Jesus and Mary. The decades begin with an Our Father and end with the Glory Be. The first five decades of the rosary are called the Joyful Mysteries, the second five the Sorrowful Mysteries, and the third five the Glorious Mysteries. The rosary has a long history, perhaps even extending to Old Testament times when Hebrews marked the recitation of the Psalms by stones or beads.

Though October is the month officially dedicated to Our Lady of the Rosary, praying the rosary during May is also a popular practice.

Finally, it is more than fitting that May, Mary's month, is also the time for the celebration of Mother's Day on the second Sunday of the month. Just as we feel called to honor our earthly mothers for the life, nurture, and love they provide us, so too do we honor our heavenly mother Mary. In the words of Pope John XXIII:

> I find it impossible not to love the holy Mother of Jesus, whom I have regarded with affection since my childhood, to whom I prayed with the first words I ever uttered, and to whom I have trustfully turned for help in the difficult moments of my life.
>
> We all find in her a tender expression of confidence and gentleness; this is a great comfort to me, a great comfort at all times.
>
> In this month of May, good Christians increase a hundredfold their tributes of profound veneration for Mary. . . .
>
> We must cherish in our hearts a fervor that will strengthen us and enable us to look to Jesus and to Our Lady with great confidence, so that we may not only await, but hasten the triumph of the Lord's love and grace, by our enthusiasm and virtuous living, and through our own special ministry.
>
> (Quoted in *Blessed Art Thou* by Richard J. Beyer, © 1996 by Ave Maria Press.)

Additional Lessons

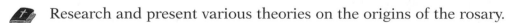 Research and present various theories on the origins of the rosary.

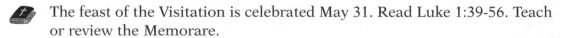 The feast of the Visitation is celebrated May 31. Read Luke 1:39-56. Teach or review the Memorare.

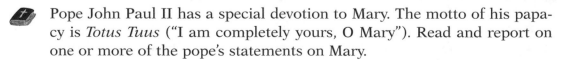 Pope John Paul II has a special devotion to Mary. The motto of his papacy is *Totus Tuus* ("I am completely yours, O Mary"). Read and report on one or more of the pope's statements on Mary.

Discussion Questions

1. What is the first thing you remember learning about Mary?
2. Describe three characteristics of the ideal mother.
3. How do you think Mary's queenship differs from the rule of earthly monarchs?

Project Ideas

Have the participants design a floral arrangement they can take home as the centerpiece of a Marian altar for their homes.

Pray five or more decades of the rosary, choosing new prayer leaders for each decade. Also, have the participants look up scripture passages to accompany each of the beads for the decades you have chosen.

The Sacrament of Confirmation

Session Topics: confirmation, commitment, creeds, ecumenical councils, Holy Spirit

Icebreaker

As the participants arrive, give each person an index card. Ask them to finish these two sentences on the index card—"I promise to . . ." and "One thing I believe is . . ."—but not sign the card. Collect the cards and pass them out randomly so that each person gets a card that is not his or her own. Then tell them to mingle around the room until they find the person who finished the two sentences. They should ask the person to explain what he or she wrote and then return the card. When everyone has his or her own card returned, gather in a large circle. Call on volunteers to share their promises and beliefs with the entire group.

Teaching

The Bostick family had rented the same cabin on the shores of Lake Michigan for the first two weeks of August for the past seventeen years. Laura, who was born in the year the Bosticks started going there, once calculated that she had spent nearly one full year of her life in the primitive two-room cabin.

On the last day of the vacation the ritual was always the same: with the cabin cleared out and the car packed, Mr. Bostick went to the front desk to return the key and pay the bill *and* to reserve the cabin again for the next summer.

But there was one part of this family ritual that Laura never did quite understand: two days before the family headed to the lake, Mr. Bostick always called to verify the reservation.

"Dad, we know we're going, they know we're coming. Why do you always have to call?" Laura wondered.

"It never hurts to confirm a promise," Mr. Bostick answered.

The sacrament of confirmation marks a time when Catholics confirm the promises made at baptism. If you were baptized as an infant, the sacrament offers you the chance to answer for yourself the promises other people (your parents and godparents) made for you years before.

What do you confirm in the sacrament of confirmation? Basically, you confirm the statements of the creed, a word that means "I believe."

Do you reject Satan and all his works and all his empty promises?

Do you believe in God the Father almighty, Creator of heaven and earth?

Do you believe in Jesus Christ, his only Son, our Lord, who was born of the Virgin Mary, was crucified, died, and was buried, rose from the dead, and is now seated at the right hand of the Father?

Do you believe in the Holy Spirit, the Lord, the giver of life, who came upon the apostles at Pentecost and today is given to you sacramentally in confirmation?

Do you believe in the holy catholic Church, the communion of saints, the forgiveness of sins, the resurrection of the body, and life everlasting?

The church has two primary creeds that include these statements, the Apostles' Creed and the Nicene Creed. The Apostles' Creed developed from the beliefs of the earliest Christian community. The Nicene Creed was issued at the ecumenical council of Nicaea in 325. An ecumenical council is a general council of all church leaders. There have been 21 ecumenical councils in church history. The most recent was the Second Vatican Council in the 1960s.

At the Second Vatican Council, the church was encouraged to recall confirmation as a sacrament of initiation, following baptism, and to celebrate it within the context of eucharist, the other sacrament of initiation.

In 1993, the United States bishops decreed that the sacrament of confirmation should be conferred sometime during the age of reason, any time from age seven to eighteen. You may be preparing for confirmation shortly, or celebrating an anniversary of confirmation this spring. Many parishes try to celebrate confirmation during the Easter season, near Pentecost, the day the Holy Spirit first came to the apostles. Confirmation deepens the gift of the Spirit that was first received at baptism as well as giving us the opportunity to confirm what we believe.

Additional Lessons

Explain symbols and elements from the rite of confirmation, including the laying on of hands, the anointing with chrism, and the presence of the bishop.

Help the participants learn and memorize the seven gifts of the Holy Spirit: wisdom, understanding, right judgment, courage, knowledge, reverence, and wonder and awe.

Research the Arian controversy, false claims about the divinity of Jesus, that was at the heart of the debate at the council of Nicaea.

Discussion Questions

1. What is something (reservation, promise, etc.) that you have formally confirmed?
2. Which creedal statement do you have the most problem understanding? What is one question you have about this statement?
3. Why do you choose (or not choose) to receive the sacrament of confirmation?

Project Ideas

Make a class banner or individual banners. Use materials like burlap, wool, drapery fabric, or corduroy and have the participants cut out symbols related to the sacrament of confirmation (e.g., dove, flames, cross, chalice, etc.). Glue the symbols on a larger piece of burlap or heavy newsprint.

Have the participants write letters to the parish's most recent confirmation class congratulating them on their full initiation into the Catholic church.

Ascension of Jesus

Session Topics: Jesus' ascension, authorship of Luke and Acts, holy days of obligation, rules of the church

Icebreaker

Arrange for each person to have a helium-filled balloon with a long ribbon and a stamped postcard addressed to the parish. The postcard should read something like this:

> The junior high students of _____ parish released several balloons heavenward in celebration of Ascension Day, the day that Jesus returned to heaven himself, and in anticipation of his eventual return in glory. Please print your name and address on this card and mail it back to us so that we can know where you found this balloon. Thank you and God bless!

Have the participants print their names on the cards and tie them to the balloon. Then take the balloons outside and launch them up to the sky. Offer a prize to the person whose balloon travels the farthest as determined by the returned postcard.

Teaching

According to the Acts of the Apostles, Jesus appeared to his disciples during the forty days after Easter. On the fortieth day, "he was lifted up, and a cloud took him from their sight" (1:9). The story of Jesus' ascension serves as a bridge between the gospel of Luke and the Acts of the Apostles, which were both written by the same author.

At certain churches and in other times, the Ascension Thursday liturgy included a procession outside of the church to a nearby hill to remind everyone that Jesus was lifted up to the sky. Also, later, the Easter candle was extinguished on Ascension Thursday to mark the end of the Easter season and the beginning of the nine-day wait until Pentecost.

The church has always celebrated this feast of the Ascension, though originally it was combined with the celebration of Pentecost. Now Ascension Thursday is a holy day of obligation in the United States, coming exactly forty days after Easter Sunday.

Attending Mass on Ascension Thursday and the other holy days of obligation (including Sundays) is one of the important rules of the church. Keeping these days holy also includes relaxing and spending time with family and avoiding unnecessary work, shopping, and the like. Three other important rules of the church which you should be familiar with and prepared to follow are:

- To lead a sacramental life. You should receive holy communion frequently, at least once a year between the first Sunday in Lent and Trinity Sunday (the Sunday after Pentecost). You should also regularly celebrate the sacrament of reconciliation, particularly any time you have committed a serious sin. In addition, you are obliged to prepare for and receive the sacrament of confirmation and, after you receive it, commit yourself in some way to spreading the gospel to others.

- To strengthen and support the church. You are obligated to support your local parish through the sharing of your time and part of your income. You must also support the pope and church worldwide through participation in the church's missionary efforts.

- To do penance and strive for holiness. You must abstain from meat and fast from food on certain days. You must also pray for and serve the poor.

Ascension Thursday is the holy day that marks the time when Jesus left the earth. Christians live in Jesus' promise that he will come again like a "thief in the night" when we least expect it. Ascension Thursday is also a preview of our own destiny in which we will someday be taken up to heaven to meet God face to face.

Additional Lessons

Compare the versions of the ascension from Acts 1:9-11, Luke 24:50-53, and Mark 16:19. Also note the similar prologues of Acts and Luke, including the literary device of addressing the writing to a named person (Theophilus).

Present church teaching on the Second Coming, especially to counteract fundamentalist teaching.

Explain the church laws in more detail. Include a study of church laws regarding marriage.

Discussion Questions

1. Why do you attend Mass when you do?
2. Do you associate Mass attendance with an "obligation"? If you do, how do you feel when you miss Mass on a Sunday or holy day?
3. If Jesus were to return to earth within one hour, what would you do to prepare for his arrival?

Project Ideas

Process to the highest point on the parish or nearby grounds (the top of a steeple or bell tower or to the top of a neighborhood bluff or hill). When you arrive, read or enact the ascension story from Acts or Luke. Then offer spontaneous prayers for personal and communal readiness for Jesus' second coming.

Collect and bag part of the food that is to be served for lunch. Plan to donate the collection to a local organization that provides food to the needy.

Pentecost

Session Topics: Pentecost, Holy Spirit, covenant, origins of the church

Icebreaker

Set a birthday cake with at least one candle in the center of a large table. Have the participants sit around the table. Before eating, explain that they will be talking about the birthday of the church. Then have them go around the table and share (1) their all-time favorite birthday party, and (2) their all-time favorite birthday present. Save the cake for dessert after lunch.

Teaching

If you were to rank your "favorite" days of the entire year, how would you do it? Some of you would probably put Christmas first: great presents, no school, Jesus' birthday, etc. The first day of summer vacation would certainly get a lot of votes. Your own birthday would have to be on the list.

Your own personal list may actually include some of the most important church feasts of the year. For example, in a strictly religious sense, the feast of the Nativity, Christmas, is certainly one of the central Christian feast days.

However, if you ranked the feast days in order, Easter would have the most importance. Easter is the day that gives meaning to our faith and distinguishes it from all others. The great joy of Jesus' resurrection translates into the possibility that we, too, will have eternal life. As St. Paul writes, "If Christ has not been raised, then empty is our preaching; empty, too, your faith" (1 Cor 15:14). In other words, your faith is worthless unless you believe Jesus is risen!

What about the *second* most important feast day? Again, Christmas doesn't necessarily fit in here. Rather, the second most important church feast day is Pentecost. St. John Chrysostom said in the fifth century about Pentecost: "Today we have arrived at the peak of all blessings, we have reached the capital of feasts, we have obtained the very fruit of the Lord's promise."

It was on Pentecost that the Holy Spirit, promised by Jesus, first came to the disciples. It is the Holy Spirit, the third person of the Blessed Trinity and truly God, that helped the early Christians to fearlessly preach the good news. Remember, prior to Jesus' death Peter and the other disciples were quavering in fear; Peter denied that he even knew Jesus. When the Holy Spirit descended on the disciples in the form of wind and fire as they hid in the upper room (the place of the last supper), they were changed into courageous souls who preached the good news strongly, and eventually were put to death for their faith just as Jesus was.

Pentecost is a Greek word that means "fiftieth day." It is celebrated fifty days after Easter. You can relate the root of the word, "pent," to other words you know that have to do with five or fifty, for example, "pentagon." The Jews also marked the fiftieth day after the Passover with a feast called the "Feast of the First Fruits" or the "Feast of Weeks." It was for this reason Jews from all over the Roman empire had gathered in Jerusalem, eventually to hear Peter's bold testimony about Jesus. The Acts of the Apostles (2:41) reports that about three thousand persons were baptized on that day.

Pentecost is often known as the "birthday" of the church because it was on this day that God's final covenant with humankind was complete. (A covenant is an agreement between two parties.) Through the coming of the Holy Spirit, the first Christians could look back on the events in the life of Jesus with new insight and see how they fit in with all that had been foretold by the prophets of the Old Testament. Stamped with the Spirit's approval, so to speak, they could now preach confidently that "Jesus is Lord!" and that Jesus was equal with the Father, true God from true God.

Additional Lessons

 Read and discuss the Pentecost narrative from Acts 2:1-41.

 Discuss what Jesus means when he calls the Holy Spirit "Paraclete." The Paraclete is literally the advocate or consoler who stands by the side of Jesus' disciples. Jesus was the first Paraclete; the Holy Spirit is the second.

 Review many of the symbols associated with the Holy Spirit (e.g., water, fire, dove). A list of the various symbols with explanations can be found in the *Catechism of the Catholic Church* (#694-701).

Discussion Questions

1. What are your three favorite days of the year? How has this list changed in the past five years?
2. When was a time you were afraid? Who or what helped you to be more courageous?
3. What is your favorite image of the Holy Spirit?

Project Ideas

Conduct this activity in a safe place. Stretch a plastic strip from a six-pack of soft drinks into one long piece. Tie one end to the middle of a wire coat hanger. Suspend the coat hanger from the ceiling. Place a large bucket of water below the plastic strip. Dim the lights. With a match, light the bottom of the plastic. "Balls of fire" simulating the tongues of fire will drop into the water. Read the Pentecost narrative or sing the mantra *Veni Sancte Spiritus* ("Come Holy Spirit") while the plastic burns.

Have the participants work individually or in small groups to do a word search through the gospel of Luke to find all of the places where the Spirit is present in Jesus' life and ministry.

Trinity Sunday

Session Topics: Trinity, Sign of the Cross, sacramental

Icebreaker

Each person should have a clear glass. Walk around the group filling each glass with water. Pause and call on a volunteer to say what is in the glass ("water"). Next, pour two tablespoons of sugar in each glass and ask someone to say what is in the glass now ("sugar water"). Then pour a small scoop of unsweetened Kool-Aid into each glass. Again, ask what they have ("Kool-Aid"). Point out how the three parts make one drink. Connect the example to the lesson on the Trinity that follows. Have everyone drink his or her Kool-Aid.

Teaching

Likely one of the first things you learned as a Catholic was how to make the Sign of the Cross. Can you remember some of your bungled efforts as a toddler of using your left hand or moving your hand from your right shoulder to your left?

Nevertheless, you did learn how to cross yourself and now the gesture is one of rote. You may make the Sign of the Cross several times a week: while offering a blessing before meals, after you dip your fingers into holy water upon entering church, twice at Mass (at the beginning and end), and at prayer before you go to sleep at night.

The Sign of the Cross is a sacramental, that is, a sacred prayer, object, or blessing. It has been a universal sign of Christianity since the very early times of the church. In the early third century, a church father, Tertullian, wrote: "At every step and movement, whenever we come in or go out, in dressing or in putting on our shoes, at the bath, at table, at the lighting of the lamps, in going to rest, in sitting down, whatever employment occupies us, we mark our foreheads with the sign of the cross" (Thurston, *Familiar Prayers*).

In earlier times, Christians made the Sign of the Cross only on their forehead, usually using only their thumb or three fingers. Eastern-rite Catholics make the Sign of the Cross from their right shoulder to their left. Catholics from Mexico and Latin American countries kiss their thumb, draped over two fingers, after making the Sign of the Cross as a sign of love and devotion to the cross itself. Before the reading of the gospel at Mass, you may make three small crosses on your forehead, lips, and heart saying to yourself: "May the word of God be in my mind, on my lips, and in my heart."

Of course the Sign of the Cross reminds us of the most central Christian mystery: the mystery of the Holy Trinity. Christians always have believed in one God, though they experienced God as three: Father, Son, and Holy Spirit. Though difficult for humans to understand, this doctrine states that though of one nature, there are three persons in God. A common understanding today is that the relationship between Father, Son, and Spirit is as a family or community of love. Their love for one another models the ultimate goal for humanity, that all people will one day love each other in the same way.

How can one God be in three persons? Again, the mystery is difficult to explain. Many images have been used to try to explain it. For example, the shamrock, though one flower, has three leaves.

The Sunday after Pentecost has become the traditional time in the church year to honor the Holy Trinity. In one of the gospel readings for that Sunday, Jesus assures us that much of the help we need to understand this and the other great mysteries of life will be left to the Spirit. Jesus said to his disciples: "I have much more to tell you, but you cannot bear it now. But when he comes, the Spirit of truth, he will guide you to all truth" (Jn 16:12-13).

Additional Lessons

Expand on these two basic explanations of the mystery of the Holy Trinity: Immanent Trinity (God-in-Godself) and Economic Trinity (God-for-us).

With Economic Trinity, help the participants assign traditional tasks to the three persons of God: for example, Father/Creator, Son/Savior, Holy Spirit/Sanctifier.

Read Ephesians 5:18-20 and 2 Corinthians 13:13. Discuss these early understandings of the doctrine of the Trinity.

Discussion Questions

1. If you were asked to explain the Trinity—one God in three persons—to a young child, how would you do it?
2. The Holy Trinity is described as a "community of love." What is a human example from your own life that helps you with this understanding of the Trinity?
3. What are concrete ways the Word of God is in your mind? on your lips? in your heart?

Project Ideas

View all or part of the video *Jesus B.C.* (Paulist Press), which provides an interesting look at the relationship between the persons of the Trinity and their actions on behalf of humankind. Discuss how the depiction of the Trinity in the video compares with the participant's understanding.

Images (like the shamrock) are only partially helpful in understanding the mystery of the Trinity. Ask the participants to work individually or in small groups to devise an image to describe the Trinity. For example, "A man is one being, yet he has three separate identities as a husband to his wife, a father to his child, and a son to his father." Allow time for the participants to share.

St. Peter and St. Paul

Session Topics: St. Peter, St. Paul, martyrdom, primacy of bishop of Rome, patron saints

Icebreaker

Hold a relay race in which two people tie their ankles together with rope, race to a certain point and back, untie their ankles, and give the rope to the next pair. Begin by dividing the participants into two teams. Have everyone in each group pair up with another person and stand next to each other in one line. Give the first pair in each line a piece of rope (approximately three feet in length). Designate the turnaround point and say "go." If the teams do not have an equal number of pairs, have one pair go an extra time.

Teaching

The next time you go on a large commercial airline flight, say a prayer for your safety and the safety of others on board. Then, just for a moment, consider what would happen if the plane you were on tragically crashed, leaving no survivors. If that did happen, you and all the people on board, mostly anonymous strangers to you, would be forevermore linked in death.

Sometimes when air tragedies like this occur, further investigation of the lives of the passengers reveals startling similarities: Perhaps two different groups of students were returning from a field trip at an historical site. Maybe there were several families with children nearly the same ages. In one recent plane crash, the lives of two famous scientists were lost; they knew of each other but had never met, and they did not even know the other was on the plane.

The point of this rather dark exercise is to show how community can be formed and people can come together even in death. This happened to two of the greatest saints in the church—Peter and Paul—who share a feast day on June 29.

St. Peter was originally named Simon when Jesus called him from his fishing boat to "come and follow me." His name appears in the New Testament more than anyone, except Jesus. Jesus left Peter the "keys of the kingdom," appointing him the first leader of the church. Peter eventually founded and led the local Christian community in Rome, but his influence and teaching were respected throughout the entire church. Since Peter, Rome has had primacy and respect in the church. The pope, Peter's successor, is the bishop of Rome.

St. Paul was once called Saul. He was a Roman citizen, a devout Pharisee (a strict Jewish sect), and a tentmaker. Paul was very skeptical of the new "way" of Christianity, going so far as to persecute Christians for their beliefs. Then, on a trip to Gaza to do just that, Paul was knocked from his horse and blinded with an appearance of the risen Christ. "Why do you persecute me?" Jesus wanted to know. Soon after, Paul's conversion became complete. He became the greatest missionary the church has ever seen, personally traveling throughout the Roman empire preaching the good news and founding many local churches. His letters to these churches are filled with inspired theology and are included in the New Testament.

But because of his faith, Paul was taken to Rome in chains as a prisoner; Christianity remained against the law in the empire.

Rome is the place where the stories of Paul and Peter come together. Tradition holds that each was murdered by the emperor Nero, some time around the year 64 A.D. Peter was crucified in the public circus or amphitheater, hung on a cross upside down in humility that he might not seem to imitate the crucifixion of Jesus. Paul was beheaded on the outskirts of the city.

A little over a century later it was rumored that Christians had taken the bodies of Peter and Paul and moved them to a common grave in the catacombs, or tunnels, below the city where Christians often gathered in hiding for prayer. An excavation of the area thought to contain the bodies in the 1920s did not find them, though interesting graffiti, written in Latin, was present. Among the written graffiti messages discovered were:

> "I, Tomius Coelius, made a feast to the honor of Peter and Paul."
> "Paul and Peter, make intercessions for me, Victor."
> "Peter and Paul, do not forget Antonius Bassus."

So, in death, these two great Christians have evermore been connected with a common feast day: Peter is the patron of fishermen (his occupation), watchmakers (the cock crowing was an early way to keep time), keymakers (he carries the keys of the kingdom), and those with fevers (Jesus healed his mother-in-law of fever). Paul is the patron of tentmakers, weavers, and theologians (he was each of these).

Additional Lessons

 Read and compare the call of Peter (Mk 1:16-17) with the call of Paul (Acts 9:1-9).

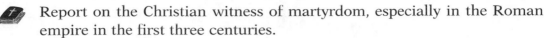

Report on the Christian witness of martyrdom, especially in the Roman empire in the first three centuries.

Share a list of careers and activities and the patron saints who go with them.

Discussion Questions

1. Who are two people you know of who are associated with one another due to their common deaths or the way they died?
2. Create a scenario where you would have enough courage to give up your life for your Christian faith.
3. Peter and Paul each left the faith of their ancestors to be Christians. Who is someone in your family who has left your religion? What reasons does this person give for doing this?

Project Ideas

Post large pieces of newsprint on more than one wall. Provide paint or colored markers. Ask the participants to write faith statements or print symbols that speak of their faith to model the graffiti found in the catacombs.

Make copies of a map of the New Testament world. Have the participants trace one, two, or all three of St. Paul's missionary journeys using the Acts of the Apostles as a reference.

Independence Day

Session Topics: Independence Day, discrimination, religious freedom, church and state

Icebreaker

Give each person a piece of paper and a pen. Tell them to move around the room collecting as many autographs as they can. The person who signs their papers must also draw a distinguishing symbol (ball, music note, car) that tells something about one of their talents or interests. After everyone has collected a fair amount of autographs, gather the group in a circle. Allow the participants to ask clarifying questions to the people who signed their papers about the talents or interests that were symbolized.

Teaching

Independence Day is not a holy day of obligation. Nevertheless, many Catholics go to Mass on the fourth of July, mainly in thanks and praise for the religious freedoms the United States allows.

But Catholics have not always enjoyed religious freedoms in the United States. At the nation's founding and in other periods of history since, Catholics were not afforded the same rights and respect as Protestants. In colonial times, for example, Catholics could not run for political offices. Catholics had to support Protestant churches with their taxes and could not build their own schools. Because of persecution, most Catholics in the New World settled in Maryland. In 1649 the Maryland colony passed the Act of Toleration, which promised religious freedom to Catholics and all other Christians. About one hundred years later, when the Puritans gained power, this law was repealed.

The prejudice and discrimination against Catholics lessened about the time of the Revolutionary War. Despite unfair treatment, most Catholics sided with the colonists because of the promise of full religious freedom. Not only were Catholic colonists among the greatest patriots in the war, but the revolution against the British was greatly helped by France, a primarily Catholic nation.

When you celebrate the anniversary of the signing of the Declaration of Independence on July 4, 1776, know that a Catholic, Charles Carroll, was the first signee. To his signature he added, "of Carrollton," to make sure all knew which Carroll was signing. The Carroll family is known as the first family of American Catholicism. Charles' cousin Daniel was a participant in the Constitutional Convention, and John Carroll was the first American bishop of the first American diocese, Baltimore. John Carroll also opened the first seminary and founded Georgetown University, the first Catholic college in America.

Nowadays, Catholics have pretty much been assimilated into American culture, though prejudice and misunderstandings still arise over positions strongly held by Catholics, for example, life issues such as abortion, capital punishment, and euthanasia. Nevertheless, the democratic government of the United States affords its citizens a chance to dissent, express opinion, protest, and participate in national issues—great graces for which all should offer thanks. The fathers of the Second Vatican Council wrote: "One must pay tribute to those nations whose systems permit the largest possible number of citizens to take part in public life in a climate of genuine freedom." Certainly the United States offers its citizens that chance.

July 4 also offers a great opportunity to celebrate life with family and friends. Cookouts, parades, camping, ball games, and fireworks are a part of the festivities: a real foretaste of the kingdom that Jesus ushered in at his coming. Enjoy the day. Remember to thank God for all of your blessings and the blessings of this nation.

Additional Lessons

Trace the family line and accomplishments of the Carroll family of Maryland, focusing on Charles, Daniel, and John Carroll.

Examine Catholicism from the perspective of various eras of United States history (e.g., Irish immigration, Ku Klux Klan, Alfred E. Smith, John F. Kennedy).

Present the "just war" doctrine (see *Catechism of the Catholic Church*, #2308) in relation to one or more wars the United States has been part of in its history.

Discussion Questions

1. What are three blessings you are thankful for as an American?
2. Many Catholic parents believe they should be given tax credit when they send their children to parochial schools. What is your opinion on this issue?

3. If you came to Sunday Mass and found the doors of the church locked, a soldier standing guard, and a sign that read, "Catholic churches closed by order of the government," how would you react?

Project Ideas

Brainstorm with the participants to develop a list of famous contemporary Catholics (e.g., actors, athletes, and politicians). Have the participants write letters asking Catholic celebrities to explain the importance of faith in their lives.

Give each participant a copy of the Bill of Rights and/or the Declaration of Independence, strips of poster paper, and a dark marker. Ask them to read the document and print relevant statements on the paper. Call on the participants to share their statements. Post the statements around the room.

St. Maria Goretti and Blessed Kateri Tekakwitha

Session Topics: St. Maria Goretti, Bl. Kateri Tekakwitha, moral decision-making, sexuality, sacredness of the body

Icebreaker

You will need at least one tape recorder for this activity. Give each participant a pencil and an index card. Tell them to compose a short message as if it would be played on a telephone answering machine. The message must succinctly tell as much as possible about what they like to do when they are away from their phones. For example, "This is Maribel. I'm not here because I'm volunteering at the veterinarian clinic." Or, "Hi, this is Alfred. I'm in the den watching the Lakers play basketball and can't be bothered." As the participants finish composing their messages, call them one at a time to have them recorded on one cassette. Play the finished cassette to the group. Call on volunteers to comment on their favorite messages.

Teaching

Saint Maria Goretti and Blessed Kateri Tekakwitha together lived a total of 35 years. Their courageous examples will no doubt live on forever. Each saint is honored in the month of July.

Maria Goretti was born in 1890 in the village of Corinaldo, near Ancona, Italy. Her family was poor. When she was nine years old, Maria's father died while her mother was pregnant with the family's sixth child. In order to survive they had to migrate as tenant farmers. Traveling with the Gorettis was a family friend, Serenelli, and his fourteen-year-old son Alessandro, whose mother had also died.

The two families came to share living space in an old barn divided into separate quarters. A statue of the Blessed Virgin was placed in the common place in the center. At age 12, Maria's job was to care for the younger children while the others worked in the fields. She didn't know how to read or write, but she had been taught the gospels and the catechism.

Alessandro became sexually attracted to Maria. He threatened her with his advances, telling her he would kill her if she told anyone about them. One day he came in early from the fields and told Maria to come inside the house from the upstairs landing where she was sewing a shirt. Maria refused. Alessandro grabbed Maria and dragged her into the kitchen area. Covering herself, she told him he would go to hell for what he was about to do. Alessandro took a sharpened knife and stabbed Maria fourteen times.

She survived for about 24 hours. During that time she forgave Alessandro. "I want him to be with me in heaven," she said.

For the murder of Maria, Alessandro was sentenced to thirty years in prison. There, he had a vision of Maria handing him flowers. His heart was changed. The first thing he did when he was released was to visit Maria's mother and beg for her forgiveness. When Pope Pius XII canonized Maria in 1950, Alessandro was at St. Peter's Square in attendance. Her feast day is July 6.

Kateri Tekakwitha was born in 1656 in an area which is now upstate New York. Her father was a Mohawk chieftain who had married her mother, Kahenta, an Algonquin, during the conquest of her tribe. What her father didn't know was that Kahenta was a Christian. She had been converted by the Jesuits and secretly prayed with a white Christian captive.

Kateri's entire family died of smallpox when she was only four years old. The disease left Kateri's faced pocked, her eyesight poor, and her legs weakened. In a culture where marriage was the ultimate goal for a woman, Kateri was shunned by her people because of her appearance. She was treated harshly and forced to do much of the menial labor for the tribe.

When her tribe allowed the Jesuit missionaries to preach to them, Kateri was attracted to the message of the gospel and was baptized. (Kateri means "Catherine.") Finally she was able to escape to Canada where she spent her last years helping the sick and elderly and living with other Christians. She died at the age of 23. Her memorial is on July 14.

In a society and culture obsessed with outward bodily appearance and sex outside of marriage, Maria Goretti and Kateri Tekakwitha represent the importance of inner beauty and moral decision-making. As St. Paul wrote: "The body, however, is not for immorality, but for the Lord, and the Lord is for the body" (1 Cor 6:13).

As you grow in your own sexuality, remember that it is a gift from God. God gave you powerful feelings that attract you to other people. God also gave you self-control to be able to act on the choices you know are right. Our bodies are God's gift to us. They are meant to give glory to God, not to bring shame.

Additional Lessons

Present a lesson on chastity, drawing especially on the material on chastity in the *Catechism of the Catholic Church*, #2331-2359. Inform and involve the parents of the teens in the planning and presentation of this material.

Assign 1 Corinthians 6:12-20 for reading. Ask the participants to consider how the description of the body as the temple of the Holy Spirit might affect the choices they make regarding their sexuality.

Explain the necessary steps for recognized sainthood, including: the informal phase, investigative phase, evaluation and judgment phase, miracle process, beatification, and canonization.

Discussion Questions

1. When was a time you feared for your life or physical safety? How was the situation resolved?
2. How important is physical and outward appearance to people in your peer group and school?
3. St. Paul wrote that the body is a "temple of the Holy Spirit." What does this mean to you?

Project Ideas

Have the participants prepare and enact role-plays that express attitudes of respect and care for their bodies and the bodies of others (e.g., exercise, avoiding alcohol, respecting others and self).

Pass out strips of paper. Ask the participants to write an expression of sorrow for their sins in this form: "I am sorry for . . . ," with one sin on each strip of paper. Allow time for them to write. Then have the participants burn the strips of paper in an urn as they offer together a prayer for forgiveness.

St. Ignatius Loyola

Session Topics: St. Ignatius Loyola, discernment, decision-making, *Spiritual Exercises*, Society of Jesus

Icebreaker

This game requires the teens to have their heads up and be on their toes. You will need a wet sponge and a large open outdoor area, preferably with a volley-ball or badminton net dividing two sides. Separate the group into two teams on both sides of the net. Explain the rules of the game: a person from one team throws the sponge *underhand* over the net. While the sponge is *in the air* the thrower yells "hands" or "toes." Someone from the other team must touch the sponge with either his or her hands or toes before it hits the ground. If the sponge hits the ground without being touched, the thrower gets to pick anyone from the other team to send out of the game. The team with the last player wins.

Teaching

Your daily life is filled with choices. In the summertime, some choices are as simple as whether you will spend the day at the swimming pool or at a friend's house. Other choices are more difficult. You may have been faced with or will soon face some of the following choices:

- To drink alcohol or not.
- To choose a college prep or vocational track of high school classes.
- To follow your parents' rules or to break curfew.
- To keep the same group of friends or to hang out with a new group.
- To have sex or to live chastely.
- To prepare for the sacrament of confirmation or to stop attending religious education.
- To go to Sunday Mass or not.

These kinds of choices are both difficult and important, and they can have life and death implications for your future. As Catholics, we believe that we are not alone in making these decisions. Jesus has left us the Holy Spirit to inspire our hearts and help us to make good and right choices.

The process of distinguishing between right and wrong, what you want and what you really need, and what is realistic and what is only an unreachable dream is known as *discernment*.

There are several discernment processes you can use when you are about to make an important decision. All of these should involve prayer. One such process can be taken from the *Spiritual Exercises* of St. Ignatius of Loyola, a former soldier who lived in Spain in the sixteenth century.

While involved in a battle, Ignatius had his leg shattered by a cannonball. The medics in the field set the leg poorly and Ignatius was forced to spend months in recovery. He found the idle time boring and asked his attendants to bring him some romance novels for reading. None of this type of book could be found. Rather, Ignatius was given books about the life of Jesus and the saints. As he read them, Ignatius was gradually transformed. On his sick bed, he made the promise that he would try to imitate the lives of the saints as much as he could once he recovered.

One of his first stops after he was well was a small town of Manresa where Ignatius made a retreat, living for a year in an outdoor cave. There he began to formulate his *Spiritual Exercises*, from which the following decision-making process is drawn. Try to use these steps when making any important decisions:

- *Pray.* Recognize God's presence in all that you do. When you pray regularly, you will easily be able to approach God for help in making a difficult choice, even when you must do so at the spur of the moment.
- *Look at All Sides of the Issue.* Make a list of pros and cons. Weigh each side. You need to consider what people you respect would say about this choice. Also consider what the church has to say.
- *Imagine Your Final Decision.* Think about the consequences if you choose the way you think you will. What would your parents say? What would a younger brother or sister think about your choice? If you are uncomfortable with the answer to either of these questions, you may be about to make a wrong choice.
- *Make Your Choice and Act.* If you have done the previous three steps, trust that God is helping you make the right choice. Act on what you have decided.
- *Evaluate Your Choice.* If you later feel a sense of satisfaction after you have acted on your choice, you have likely made a good choice. Ask yourself if your relationship with God and others has improved or worsened because of the choice you made.

Others became attracted to the *Spiritual Exercises* of St. Ignatius, and eventually, with ten other men, he formed the "Company of Jesus," whose mission was to be of service to the pope. Today, the Society of Jesus, or Jesuits, is the largest religious order in the Catholic church and is the sponsor of many high schools and colleges. St. Ignatius' feast day is on July 31.

Additional Lessons

From a book about the lives of the saints, read a short biography of St. Ignatius Loyola to the participants.

Give real-life examples from the choice categories listed above. Take the participants through the discernment process to help them see how to make a good choice in that situation.

Define sin, including definitions of serious (mortal) sin and lesser (venial) sin, especially as they apply to the issues mentioned above.

Discussion Questions

1. How can one or more of the choices described in this lesson have life and death implications?
2. What is a difficult decision you made recently? How did you go about deciding as you did?
3. How would you finish this sentence: "I promise to make a commitment to Christ by . . ."?

Project Ideas

Give each participant a blank map of the United States. As you name each Jesuit college (e.g., Loyola of Chicago, University of San Francisco), have the participants print the names of the colleges in the correct place on the map.

Distribute wallet-size index cards. Have the participants print the decision-making steps listed above on the cards. Tell them to keep them handy for reference when making a decision.

Transfiguration of Jesus

Session Topics: transfiguration, discipleship, identity of Jesus

Icebreaker

Conduct a "mini" trust walk. You will need one blindfold (e.g., torn pieces of sheet) for every two participants. Give blindfolds to half the participants and have them put them on. While they are doing this, give directions to the other half about how to lead their partners and the area they may use. Suggest that they include experiences such as smelling a flower, going up a step, catching a ball, or tasting a cookie. Allow five to ten minutes. Then repeat the process as the participants switch roles.

Teaching

Do you know what means it to "blindly follow"? Perhaps this phrase conjures up for you an image of sheep, who will "blindly" follow a lead sheep up a ramp to the very edge of the electrocution device used to slaughter them.

In the gospels of Matthew, Mark, and Luke, Jesus calls Peter, James, John, and the other apostles to follow him. The gospels don't really explain why other than to say that Jesus promised to make them "fishers of men." This seems a rather strange and unclear promise.

As the gospels proceed, the meaning of discipleship (from the Greek word for "learner") becomes more clear. Peter guesses that Jesus is the Messiah, or Chosen One, whom the Hebrew prophets had spoken of. Jesus doesn't deny this, and he explains further that he is the suffering Messiah and that his mission is to suffer greatly, be rejected by his own people, arrested, killed—and then rise three days later. He also adds that they, as disciples, can expect the same fate.

Whoa. This was a shock to the fishermen who had left their boats to follow him. Suffering and death was not what they had in mind. When Peter complains, Jesus tells him, "You are thinking not as God does; but as human beings do" (Mk 8:33).

Each of the gospels follows Jesus' passion prediction with the account of his transfiguration. (*Transfigure* means "to change in outward appearance.")

The transfiguration occurred on a high mountain, maybe Mount Tabor or Mount Hermon. According to the gospel of Mark, Jesus' "clothes became dazzling white, such as no fuller on earth could bleach them" (9:3). Jesus balanced the dire predictions of the suffering he and they would have to endure with a glimpse of the glorious resurrection that was also in their futures.

Two great people in Jewish ancestry appear with Jesus: the prophet Elijah and Moses. Moses, who had given the Chosen People the Law, was there to honor Jesus, as was Elijah, who had called the people back to follow the Law after they had ignored it while living in exile.

God the Father's voice is heard confirming Jesus as his Son. A cloud comes over the mountain, reminding Peter, James, and John of the cloud that led the wandering Israelites on their pilgrimage through the desert.

Peter and the others, in a typical human reaction, want to build booths or statues on the site to honor the occasion. He says to Jesus: "It is good that we are here!"

The gospel story of the transfiguration is read on the second Sunday of Lent. The feast of the Transfiguration, however, is on August 6. Traditionally, it was believed that the transfiguration occurred forty days before the crucifixion. Rather than marking the feast in Lent, the day is a full forty days before the feast of the Holy Cross on September 14.

The transfiguration can teach you a lot about how Jesus feels about you, a disciple. Though you, too, may have trouble understanding him and his mission, or shy away when pain and suffering come your way, Jesus is ready to remind you of your ultimate destiny, that day you will live with him in eternity.

When you are with Jesus can you easily say, like Peter, "how good it is to be with you"?

Additional Lessons

Read and compare the three accounts of the transfiguration from Matthew 17:1-13, Mark 9:2-13, and Luke 9:28-36. As an example of their differences, only in Luke is the topic of conversation between Jesus, Moses, and Elijah revealed (see Lk 9:31).

Read the stories of Elijah and the widow (1 Kgs 17) and Elijah and the prophets of Baal (1 Kgs 18) as background on the significance of this Old Testament prophet appearing with Jesus.

On a map of the New Testament world, point out Mount Tabor and Mount Hermon, noting the proximity to Caesarea Philippi, the region where Jesus and his disciples were reported to be traveling.

Discussion Questions

1. Who is someone (e.g., a popular peer) or what is something (e.g., a new fad) that you have "blindly" followed? What were the results?
2. Why do you think people tend to want to build permanent memorials for famous people and events? What is such a memorial that you have seen or know about?
3. Jesus offered Peter, James, and John a "glimpse of heaven." When have you been given a glimpse of heaven? What was it like?

Project Ideas

Write the phrase "How good it is to be here" on the board. Ask the participants to brainstorm a long list of their favorite places. Write them on the board. Use the ideas as a starting point for a discussion on how God can be found in our favorite places.

Give each participant a piece of art paper and a choice of several art supplies: felt tip pens, paints, pencils. Have them draw their impressions of the transfigured Jesus. Display the finished drawings in the room, allowing everyone the chance to look at the different impressions.

August

Assumption of Mary

Session Topics: assumption of Mary, papal infallibility, resurrection of the body, dogma, respect for the body

Icebreaker

Divide the participants into groups with about four to six people in each group. Give each group a pad of paper and a pencil. Tell them that when you say "go" you are going to ask them to brainstorm a list of items having to do with summer. The group with the most items on its list wins the game. Set a time limit for brainstorming at five minutes. Possible list of summer-related items: (1) names of amusement parks; (2) names of popular current songs; (3) names of students who will be entering sixth grade in the next term; (4) names of cities in Florida; (5) names of commercial airlines; (6) names of ice cream flavors; etc.

Teaching

In the United States and in many other countries, August 15, the feast of the Assumption of the Virgin Mary into heaven, is a holy day of obligation.

The assumption was when Mary's body was assumed or taken up to heaven through the power of God to be with her son, Jesus. By declaring that the assumption was a dogma of faith, Pope Pius XII was only confirming what the people of the church had believed for centuries. (A dogma is a recognized doctrine to be held in faith by the entire church. When Pope Pius declared the dogma of the assumption, he did so *ex cathedra*, that is, "from the chair" of Peter, assuring that it was infallible.)

An annual feast day on August 15 to honor Mary is thought to have been celebrated in the Holy Land as early as the sixth century. A bishop of that era wrote about a celebration on the anniversary of Mary's "falling asleep." The Eastern church named the feast the "Falling Asleep of the Mother of God."

The dogma of the assumption holds that Mary's body, born without original sin, was incorruptible and was taken to heaven after her death. The assumption of Mary has been included in many legends and stories. In the fifth century, at the famous Council of Chalcedon, the Eastern Roman emperor asked the Bishop of Jerusalem to have the relics of Mary's body brought to Constantinople. The bishop is said to have responded, "Mary died in the presence of the apostles; but her tomb, when opened later on the request of St. Thomas, was found empty, and thus the apostles concluded that the body was taken up to heaven."

Mary was the first disciple of her son, and her assumption is a preview of our own fate after death. Christians believe in the resurrection of the body and soul. As the *Catechism of the Catholic Church* teaches: "God, in his almighty power, will definitively grant incorruptible life to our bodies by reuniting them with our souls, through the power of Jesus' Resurrection" (#997).

In the First Letter to the Corinthians (15:40-44), St. Paul describes the attributes of our heavenly bodies as imperishable, glorious, powerful, and spiritual. In heaven, we will never die again. He writes:

> There are both heavenly bodies and earthly bodies, but the brightness of the heavenly is one kind and that of the earthly another. The brightness of the sun is one kind, the brightness of the moon another, and the brightness of the stars another. For star differs from star in brightness.
>
> So also is the resurrection of the dead. It is sown corruptible; it is raised incorruptible. It is sown dishonorable; it is raised glorious. It is sown weak; it is raised powerful. It is sown a natural body; it is raised a spiritual body. If there is a natural body, there is also a spiritual one.

The feast of the Assumption is a reminder to you to take care of your body and respect it as a Temple of the Holy Spirit, for it is the seed from which your eternal heavenly body will some day blossom.

Additional Lessons

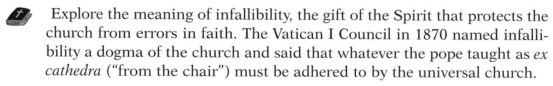

Explore the meaning of infallibility, the gift of the Spirit that protects the church from errors in faith. The Vatican I Council in 1870 named infallibility a dogma of the church and said that whatever the pope taught as *ex cathedra* ("from the chair") must be adhered to by the universal church.

As the *Catechism of the Catholic Church* states, after we die "we shall not return to our earthly lives . . . . There is no 'reincarnation' after death" (#1013). Help the participants to understand the church's position against reincarnation and for the resurrection of the body.

Examine in more detail the characteristics of the heavenly body as described by St. Paul: imperishable, glorious, powerful, and spiritual.

Discussion Questions

1. Outline a workable program of diet and exercise you plan to take as an adult to show respect and care for your own body.
2. How do you imagine your own heavenly body? What "age" do you think you will be in heaven?
3. Do you think it is important for the church to speak infallibly on certain matters of faith? Which ones? Why?

Project Ideas

The fourth glorious mystery of the rosary is a meditation on the assumption of Mary. Have the participants choose scripture verses from Song of Songs (especially chapter 2) and the book of Revelation (especially chapters 11 and 12) that can be recited along with a Hail Mary for each bead. Pray this decade of the scriptural rosary together, calling on participants to read one or more of the passages they have chosen.

Have the participants work in small groups to design the "perfect" person, making sure to include the following attributes: physical, intellectual, social, spiritual, emotional, and gender. Give each group a large piece of newsprint and have them draw and/or list traits for each of these categories. Allow time for representatives of each group to share their finished work with everyone.

St. Monica and St. Augustine

Session Topics: St. Monica, St. Augustine, parenthood, prayer, conversion, scholarship, doctor of the church

Icebreaker

Tell the participants that one focus of today's teaching is the tug in each person's soul between following or not following Christ, between good or evil. Then, engage in an old-fashioned tug of war, evenly pairing up two teams on different sides of a rope. To increase the challenge, add another rope and play simultaneously with four teams. (As if positioned on a clock, the team at 12 o'clock will oppose the team at 6 o'clock and the team at 3 o'clock will oppose the team at 9 o'clock.) Continue the competition until one team emerges as a winner.

Teaching

On August 27 and 28, the feast days of two Catholic saints—mother and son—are celebrated back to back. It figures.

St. Monica could be called the "persistent mother." A North African woman living in the fourth century, Monica was married to Patricus, a pagan, through the arrangement of her family. Monica endured plenty of emotional abuse from her husband, but her greater challenge was her oldest son, Augustine.

When he was a child, Monica taught her son the Catholic catechism and how to pray. When Augustine grew seriously ill, he requested baptism; but when he began to recover, the baptism was forgotten.

Later, as a student in Carthage, Augustine came to follow a heretical teaching that claimed that the body was evil while the soul alone was good. He also like to party, and he lived with his girlfriend and their son. Monica was so disgusted with Augustine that she would not let him eat or sleep in her home.

Mother and son rarely talked. Still, Monica continued to pray for Augustine after a bishop told her that it was better to talk to God about Augustine than to Augustine about God. The bishop also told her: "At present the heart of the young man is too stubborn, but God's time will come. It is not possible that the son of so many tears should perish."

Augustine's time came some years later. In Milan, Augustine was inspired by the preaching of the Catholic bishop, St. Ambrose. Soon after, Augustine became torn between living chastely and his past sinfulness. Augustine went out to an outer garden at the place where he was staying. He threw himself on the ground under a tree and cried out, "How long, O Lord? Will you always be angry with me? Remember not my past sins."

Just then Augustine could hear the singing of a neighbor child on the other side of the wall. The child kept repeating the same verse over and over, "Tolle lege! Tolle lege!" which means, "Take up and read!" He got up, went inside, and found the Bible sitting on a table. Augustine randomly opened the Bible to Romans 13 where he read: "Let us then throw off the works of darkness and put on the armor of light; let us conduct ourselves properly as in the day, not in orgies and drunkenness, not in promiscuity and licentiousness, not in rivalry and jealousy. But put on the Lord Jesus Christ, and make no provision for the desires of the flesh" (13:12-14).

Augustine was baptized by Ambrose on Easter Sunday in 387. Soon after, his mother died. She said shortly before her death, "I do not know what there is now left for me to do or why I am still here. All I wished to live for was that I might see you a Catholic and a child of heaven."

Augustine lived chastely from that time on. He was ordained and named bishop of Hippo. St. Augustine is one of the great scholars of the church. He is a doctor of the church, an honorary title given to great leaders, writers, scholars, and teachers of the early centuries.

His mother has not been forgotten either. St. Monica is the patron saint of mothers and fathers and of all lost and wayward children. And, the church recently moved St. Monica's feast day to August 27 so that it would be near her son's the following day.

Additional Lessons

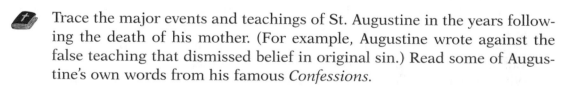

Trace the major events and teachings of St. Augustine in the years following the death of his mother. (For example, Augustine wrote against the false teaching that dismissed belief in original sin.) Read some of Augustine's own words from his famous *Confessions*.

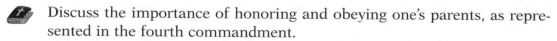

Discuss the importance of honoring and obeying one's parents, as represented in the fourth commandment.

St. Monica practiced intercessory prayer on behalf of her son. Intercessory prayer is prayer that looks not only to one's own interests, but also to the interests of others. Explore this definition further, especially from the *Catechism of the Catholic Church*, #2634-2636.

Discussion Questions

1. When was a time that your parents embarrassed you? How did you let them know you were embarrassed?
2. If you asked your parents to tell the one dream they have for you, what do you think they would say?
3. What is one area of your life that you wish you could change? What is one step you can take to begin to make this change?

Project Ideas

Give each person a bible. Ask them to randomly open to any page, as Augustine once did. Encourage a period of quiet meditation. Then go around the group asking each person to tell which words, verses, or longer passages spoke to them on the pages they opened to.

Have the participants write a story about a person they know who, as St. Augustine once did, needs conversion to a Christian lifestyle. Tell the participants to use a fictitious name in their writing. When they are finished, collect all the stories and read some of them aloud.

Mother Teresa of Calcutta

Session Topics: Mother Teresa, vocation, service to the poor

Icebreaker

Give each person three strips of paper (approximately 1" x 5"). Have them finish the following sentences, one on each strip:

"A time I experienced God calling me was . . . ."

"The worst poverty I know of is . . . ."

"I can serve others by . . . ."

Collect the finished strips of paper. Read a sampling of each type of finished sentence to the group.

Teaching

Agnes Boyaxhui heard two distinct calls to serve God. As a teenager, she left her homeland of Yugoslavia for Ireland and the Sisters of Loretto. From there she was sent to India to do her novitiate, where she was a schoolteacher for the next eighteen years.

Then, in 1946, the Lord spoke clearly to her again while she was on her way to retreat. "I heard the call to give up all and to follow him into the slums and to serve among the poorest of the poor," she said.

She left her sisters and pledged herself to the bishop of Calcutta, India, and to the poorest and sickest of that city. In 1952 she found a dying woman on the streets, her body becoming a feast for ants and rats. The hospital did not have room for the woman. A city official offered an abandoned building as shelter for this dying woman and the thousands who would come after her.

Agnes is better known as Mother Teresa, the founder of the Missionaries of Charity, who dedicate themselves to serving the poorest of the poor.

Mother Teresa died on September 5, 1997. Her example of love for the "least brothers and sisters" of this world left a mark on a twentieth-century culture known for excess and consumerism. She spoke many times of the importance of love and family, of accepting the gift of life, and of learning many lessons from the poor.

One of her favorite stories was of a man she and her sisters picked up from the street drain, half eaten by worms. When they brought him to their home, the man said, "I have lived like an animal in the street, but am going to die as an angel: loved and care for."

Mother Teresa was honored many times in her life. In 1979 she won the Nobel Peace Prize. In 1992 she was asked to come to New York to be presented with $100,000 for her work by a Catholic organization. The occasion was a fancy formal dinner where filet mignon would be served. Mother Teresa accepted the check. Next she scolded the crowd for their extravagance, telling them that before she came it took her three hours to scrape the maggots from a dying man's body. Then she left without eating. A few days later, she received another $100,000 donation, equal to the cost of the banquet.

What was so attractive about Mother Teresa to many people was that she "walked the talk." For example, visitors to her chapel in Calcutta would notice that the lights were turned off during all of the parts of the Mass except when there was a reading. "No money that is given to the poor should be wasted on our electricity. We use only what we absolutely need," she explained.

Her life was an answer to the challenge extended by Jesus that whatever is done for the hungry, the thirsty, the lonely, and the naked was done for him. As Mother Teresa explained:

> At the end of life we will not be judged by
>> how many diplomas we have received
>> how much money we have made
>> how many great things we have done.
>
> We will be judged by
>> "I was hungry and you gave me to eat
>> I was naked and you clothed me
>> I was homeless and you took me in."
>> (*Words to Love By*, Ave Maria Press)

Additional Lessons

Read Matthew 25:31-45. Ask the participants to suggest people who fit into the categories of "least brothers and sisters" in their school, local community, and world at large.

Present more information on the life of Mother Teresa, especially from articles in several periodicals written at the time of her death in September 1997. If possible, make copies of the articles so that the participants can read along.

Teach the spiritual and corporal works of mercy.

Discussion Questions

1. When have you felt "called" by God to do something for God or for people in need?
2. Do you think Mother Teresa was right or wrong for refusing to eat at the banquet with the people who honored her? Explain.
3. Who are people at your school or in your community who need to have someone reach out to them because of their material or spiritual needs? What could you do for these people?

Project Ideas

Have the participants walk in pairs in a place where they can pass by many different people (e.g., around the block, at a shopping center). Tell them to have one person approach someone and say "hello" while the other person observes the person's reaction (surprise, friendliness, sullenness, etc.). Repeat the exercise several times, switching roles as time allows. Discuss the various reactions with the entire group.

View all or part of a video on the life of Mother Teresa. Vision and Values (800-233-4629) offers a video *Mother Teresa* by Ann and Jeanette Petrie and narrated by Richard Attenborough.

The Holy Cross

Session Topics: the cross, resurrection, capital punishment, relics

Icebreaker

Play a game so that everyone can learn each other's names. Ask everyone to think of an adjective that describes him or her and also begins with the same sound as the first letter of his or her first name; for example, "Mischievous Mike" or "Energetic Ellen." Sit in a circle. Choose one person to share his or her adjective and name. The next person repeats the first person's adjective and name and shares his or her own adjective and name. The third person repeats the adjectives and names of the first two people and tells his or her own. Continue the process all the way around the circle. Allow neighbors to help anyone who gets stuck.

Teaching

Can you imagine going into your church and seeing an electric chair hanging from the ceiling or hung prominently on the wall behind the altar? Or, could you see yourself wearing a chain with a medal depicting the image of a gas chamber? How about making a sign with your hands as if you were tying a hangman's noose before beginning your prayers?

If you think these mental images are crazy, then you should feel the same any time you see a crucifix hung in a church, wear a cross around your neck, or make the Sign of the Cross before you pray.

Crucifixion by the cross was as violent or more violent than any of the forms of capital punishment our society uses today.

Actually, the Romans had two forms of crucifixion at the time of Jesus. Roman citizens were beheaded. Foreigners like Jesus were forced to carry a single

117

crossbeam outside the walls of the city to a place called Golgotha (Skull Place) where the upright posts were permanently fixed. Many times the weight of the crossbeam alone would kill the person; in Jesus' case he was so weakened by the beatings and abuse he had absorbed that another man, Simon of Cyrene, was permitted to help him carry it.

Once hung or tied on the cross, Roman soldiers often would break the legs of the condemned. This did not happen to Jesus. Sometimes a soldier would lance the person's side to hasten death. In Jesus' case, when his side was lanced—and water flowed out with blood—he was already dead.

Only John's gospel mentions that Jesus was nailed to the cross. This practice, too, is confirmed by archaeological finds. It seems the Romans had refined this torture so that the cross included a small seat, called the *seidle*, where the accused could support just one buttock while the spikes were driven through the hands and feet. The torture was unbearable. Besides the obvious pain, insects were attracted to the open wounds, and Jesus would have been unable to shoo them away.

The cross is a great paradox, or contradiction, because out of this misery of death is new life for all who are baptized and believe in Christ. As St. Paul wrote: "The message of the cross is foolishness to those who are perishing, but to us who are being saved it is the power of God" (1 Cor 1:18).

The feast of the Holy Cross is celebrated on September 14. It is believed that this is the day in 335 the emperor Constantine dedicated the Church of the Holy Sepulcher over the site at Golgotha where Jesus died. Reportedly, Constantine's mother, St. Helena, had traveled to Golgotha and found not only Christ's cross, but those of the two thieves crucified next to him. The three crosses were then taken to the house of a dying woman where the true cross of Christ restored her to health.

By 346 the relics of the cross discovered by St. Helena were on their way to different parts of the world. Part of the cross was placed in a statue of Constantine in the newly-built city of Constantinople. More of the cross was subdivided and placed in church altars. (It used to be required that each altar have a holy relic, for example, the bones of a saint or martyr. Nowadays this is not a requirement as altars are seen to be dedicated to God alone. However, many church altars still have relics.)

As you pass near a cross in the next days and weeks, rethink its original meaning and the brutal form of death that Jesus suffered on your behalf.

Additional Lessons

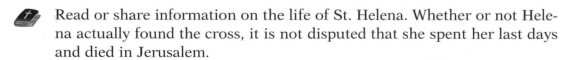

Read or share information on the life of St. Helena. Whether or not Helena actually found the cross, it is not disputed that she spent her last days and died in Jerusalem.

Explain the church's current position on capital punishment. See, for example, Pope John Paul II's 1995 encyclical, *Evangelium Vitae* ("The Gospel of Life"), especially no. 56.

Provide information on the altar relics at your church or at a neighboring church. If possible, have the participants view the vault where the relics are stored.

Discussion Questions

1. What do you think was the worst pain that Jesus experienced?
2. What would you say to a convicted murderer to convince him or her of the dignity of human life?
3. What is your opinion on capital punishment as a deterrent to crime?

Project Ideas

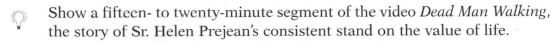 Show a fifteen- to twenty-minute segment of the video *Dead Man Walking*, the story of Sr. Helen Prejean's consistent stand on the value of life.

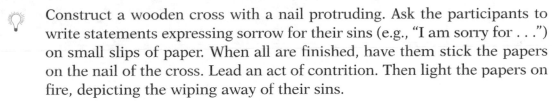 Construct a wooden cross with a nail protruding. Ask the participants to write statements expressing sorrow for their sins (e.g., "I am sorry for . . .") on small slips of paper. When all are finished, have them stick the papers on the nail of the cross. Lead an act of contrition. Then light the papers on fire, depicting the wiping away of their sins.

September / October

Archangels and Guardian Angels

Session Topics: angels, Michael, Gabriel, Raphael, faith in the unseen, idolatry, superstition, divination, sorcery or magic

Icebreaker

You will need at least three separate televisions and VCRs. Set up each in separate corners of the room. Play different videos that contain an "angel" theme: for example, *Angels in the Outfield, Michael, Heaven Can Wait,* or *It's A Wonderful Life.* As the participants arrive, tell them to gather around the TV of their choice. After everyone has watched a little of a video, gather the group together and have them summarize the plot, what they liked about that story, and how the story represents angels or spiritual beings.

Teaching

There are two Catholic feasts honoring angels at the end of September and the beginning of October. The first, on September 29, is the feast of the Archangels. Archangels are the only "named" angels in all of scripture; they are Michael, Gabriel, and Raphael.

Raphael is mentioned in the book of Tobit as an aide to Tobiah, the son of Tobit, as he retrieves a fish that will heal his father's blindness. Gabriel is the angel in Luke 1:26 who announces to Mary that she will be the mother of God's son. September 29 was originally the sole feast of St. Michael, for it was on this day that a Mass and church in Rome were first dedicated to him. Michael is cited most often in the books of Daniel and Revelation as a defender against evil.

Just who are angels and what does the church believe about them? The church holds that angels are spiritual beings who were created by God prior to the creation of the universe. Though without bodies, angels have free will and a naturally superior intellect to humans. The word angel means "messenger." As in the examples from scripture, the angels prayerfully watch over people. In the New Testament angels assisted Jesus and his disciples.

God made angels joyful and good, but some angels turned away from God and were banished to hell. Satan, also known as Lucifer, is believed to be one of the "bad angels." The bad angels, or devils, are able to tempt us to sin. In the same way, good angels personally watch out for us. Since about the third century, the church has maintained, though not officially, that all the baptized have guardian angels who personally watch out for them. The feast of the Guardian Angels is celebrated on October 2.

The existence of angels recalls for us the creedal statement we pray each Sunday at Mass: "We believe in what is seen and unseen." Angels are part of God's unseen creation whose vocation is to serve God's will. In recent years, many people not previously in touch with spirituality or religion have been attracted to angels.

Remember that angels can be honored as with all the saints, but never worshipped; only God is deserving of our adoration and worship. The first commandment says that you should put nothing before God. When this happens, it is a form of idolatry, that is, the worship of idols. Satanism or "devil worship" is the most serious type of idolatry. Related worship and practices contrary to the first commandment are:

Superstition—giving magical importance to certain actions or things.

Divination—attempting to predict the future through horoscopes, astrology, palm reading, fortune tellers. Even playing the Ouija board falls under this category because it implies the conjuring up of spirits to reveal a truth. Only God can reveal truth.

Magic or sorcery—attempting to tame devils or occult powers in order to have them at one's service.

St. Michael is especially called upon to defend us against evil and evil spirits. The following prayer is addressed to him:

> Holy Michael the Archangel, defend us in battle.
> Be our protection against the wickedness and snares of the devil.
> May God rebuke him, we humbly pray,
> and do thou, O Prince of the heavenly host, by the power of God,
> thrust into hell Satan and all wicked spirits
> who wander through the world for the ruin of souls.

Additional Lessons

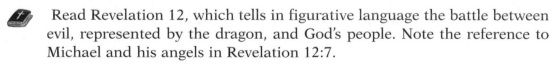 Read Revelation 12, which tells in figurative language the battle between evil, represented by the dragon, and God's people. Note the reference to Michael and his angels in Revelation 12:7.

Cover in more detail the church's teaching on the existence of angels from the *Catechism of the Catholic Church*, #328-336.

The discussion on Satanism may lead to a question about the church's practice of exorcisms. Number 1673 in the *Catechism* provides a point of reference.

Discussion Questions

1. What do you believe about angels?
2. What forms of idolatry have you or someone you know practiced? What do you perceive are the dangers of the examples of idolatry described here?
3. If you could be an angel for a day, what are some things you would like to do?

Project Ideas

Call on two participants to volunteer for an improvisation. One person takes the role of the guardian angel for the other. The two dialogue with one another, asking questions about each other's actions, behaviors, and goals. Another option is for the participants to write letters to their guardian angels, querying them about their purpose. Share some of the finished letters with the group.

The video *It's a Wonderful Life* depicts well the role of a guardian angel. Have the participants help you to re-create the story. Show more of the video.

St. Thérèse of Lisieux

Session Topics: St. Thérèse, humility, vocation, conversion

Icebreaker

Divide the participants into small groups. Give each group a piece of newsprint marked with a time line covering the next twenty years of their lives and marked in five-year intervals. Also distribute crayons or colored markers to each group. Tell the participants to print words or symbols near specific ages on the time line to show how they imagine their lives in those years. When everyone has printed something, go around the group and ask one question that seeks clarification of the meaning of a symbol or word.

Teaching

You live in a time when teenagers have achieved worldly riches and glory. Young athletes, just graduated from high school, sign multi-million dollar contracts. Other teenagers with just the "right" look are discovered by talent agents and set up to be the next supermodels.

Do the fulfilled dreams of these teenagers in any way parallel your own? What do you hope to achieve for yourself in high school? If you could look into the future twenty years, what kind of life do you imagine for yourself?

There was a young teenage girl who lived in Lisieux, France, in the late nineteenth century who also had big dreams. Thérèse Martin knew from an early age that she wanted *everything* God had to offer.

When Thérèse was two years old, her older sister Leonie held up a dress-making kit to Thérèse and her six-year-old sister Celine. "Take what you want," the older girl offered. Celine politely took a small woolen ball. Thérèse reached out and took the entire kit. "I choose all," she said.

Thus, the pattern of her life was established early; Thérèse never did anything half-heartedly. By the time she was thirteen, Thérèse was convinced of something she had felt for years: that she wanted to devote her life to God, especially in prayer for the conversion of sinners. She asked God for a sign that this was his will for her. At that time, a murderer in her area had been sentenced to die by guillotine. The man showed no signs that he would repent. Thérèse offered daily prayers for his conversion. On the day after he was executed, Thérèse read in the newspaper that he had grabbed the crucifix of the chaplain standing nearby and kissed it three times before he was beheaded. Thérèse took this to mean that God was pleased with her decision.

Thérèse had to petition the local bishop to allow her entrance into the Carmelite convent when she was only 15. In fact, she even went to the pope, blurting out her request to him while on a pilgrimage with her parish.

Thérèse was barely distinguishable as a sister. Yet, she had devised a symbol for her life. She was like a little flower that survives the harshest conditions of winter only to appear again in the spring. Her goal was to go to heaven. She recalled that "heaven" was the first word she learned to read. She loved Sundays because she felt they were a glimpse of heaven and dreaded Sunday nights as the feeling slipped away. "I long for the everlasting repose of heaven," she said.

Thérèse's plan to achieve heaven was, in her words, "the little way." She offered all of the "little" events of her day to Jesus: the daily cleaning and laundry work; the impatience she had with an older nun who always made a clacking noise with her rosary when she prayed.

Thérèse contracted tuberculosis on Good Friday in 1896. Her last two years were filled with physical and mental suffering. She died when she was only 24.

No one would have known about the intense relationship Thérèse had formed with Jesus and her devotion to the little way if she hadn't written her biography, at the request of her sister Pauline, the prioress of the convent.

October 1 is the feast day of the Little Flower, canonized a saint in 1925. In 1997, Pope John Paul II named Thérèse a doctor of the church. Her intercessions are no doubt felt in many ways on earth. In her biography, *The Story of a Soul*, Thérèse wrote, "How happy shall I be in heaven if I cannot do favors on earth for those whom I love?"

Additional Lessons

Thérèse was the youngest of nine children of Louis Martin and Zeilie Guerin. Four of the children died when they were young. Find and share more details of Thérèse's life.

As Thérèse exemplified, the church believes that indulgences can be gained for others through works and prayer, including for those souls in purgatory. Explore this understanding of indulgences with the participants.

Present more information on religious vocations, especially as "a calling" from God. If possible, contact the vocation director of a local religious community for information on their process for welcoming novices.

Discussion Questions

1. How was Thérèse's idea of success different from what many people desire today?
2. If you said to God, "I want all," what would your all be?
3. Describe one incident in the past week in which you lived Thérèse's little way.

Project Ideas

Have the participants begin a prayer diary, focusing on events in their lives they can offer to God in the spirit of Thérèse's little way.

St. Thérèse of Lisieux's symbol was the Little Flower. Her motto for life was the "little way." Give each participant a piece of poster board and some art supplies. Ask them to design a symbol and motto for their own lives. Display the finished posters where all can see.

St. Francis of Assisi

Session Topics: St. Francis, vocation, poverty, relationships between parents and children

Icebreaker

You will need at least one roll of toilet paper. (To be on the safe side, have an extra roll available.) Have all the participants sit in one circle. Show them a large roll of toilet paper. Tell the group that you are going to pass around the roll and that everyone should take as many sheets as they want. (Each person should take at least one sheet.) After the roll has been around the circle explain to the group that they must tell something about themselves for every sheet they took. Some people may have to only tell one thing; others will have to tell many things!

Teaching

You may know of several friends or acquaintances who deviated from the plans their parents had for them. Perhaps you've seen situations like these:

- the coach's son who no longer likes sports;
- the doctor's daughter who gags at the sight of blood;
- the business owner's children who revolt at working in the family business.

This final example comes closest to describing the troubles Peter Bernardone had with his son, Francis.

A rich, clothing merchant living in Assisi, Italy, in the early thirteenth century, Peter planned for his son to work with him and eventually succeed him in business. About the age of 20, Francis began to move off course.

First, he joined the military. As a knight, he fought in one losing battle for Assisi, was captured by the opposing army, and kept in a dungeon for several months. When he finally returned home, Francis' mother and father spoiled him more than ever. His dad gave him money to spend and encouraged Francis to recuperate by partying in the evenings with his boyhood friends. Once healed, Francis grew restless again and headed to southern Italy to continue his military career. On one of his first nights away, as Francis camped in a desolate spot, he heard a voice ask him, "Who can do more for you, the servant or the master?" Francis answered, "The master, of course." The voice responded, "Then why are you devoting your life to the servant?"

Francis understood the "Master" to be a reference to Christ, and he returned home.

From that point on the parties didn't have the same excitement for Francis. His friends assumed he must be in love and planning to marry. "Who is she?" one of them questioned as Francis stood out on a balcony gazing up to the sky. "She whom I shall marry is so noble, so rich, so fair and so wise, that not one of you has seen her like," he answered. Francis was talking about Lady Poverty, to whom he would soon make a lifelong commitment while taking retreat in a nearby mountain cave.

Things were now happening rapidly to Francis. Soon after making his promise, Francis passed by an old chapel, St. Damian, on the outskirts of town. Again, Francis heard a voice: "Go and repair my church, which as you can see is falling into ruin."

Francis took the message literally, not realizing that he would eventually help to repair the worldwide Catholic church. Francis usually would ask his father for money, but his father was out of town, so Francis took some of his best cloth materials and exchanged them for gold. He then went back to St. Damian's and began his restoration work. (The priest there refused his money.)

Peter Bernardone was furious when he discovered what Francis had done. He retrieved Francis and had him chained in his cellar. Only when Peter went on another business trip did Francis' mother release him. He went back to St. Damian's and completed his work.

Finally, when Francis showed up again in town, Peter had his son arrested. Francis would agree only to a trial before the local bishop. When the bishop told Francis to pay his father back, Francis not only gave him his money, but he stripped himself of his clothes and left them right in the middle of the town square. "Now I will be able to call God my Father, not Peter Bernardone," Francis told everyone.

Eventually, Francis' love for Lady Poverty attracted eleven other men from Assisi to follow him. There were thousands of Franciscans by the time of his death, including a Franciscan order for women founded by his friend, St. Clare. Whether Francis eventually reconciled with his father, we do not know.

We do know that the sincerity of St. Francis' life has won many converts in the years since he lived on earth. He is one of the most popular of all saints, and his feast day is October 4.

Additional Lessons

 Cover other important events in the life of St. Francis, for example, his encounter with a leper, the organization of the Franciscans, his friendship with St. Clare, his meeting with the pope, his missionary trip to Egypt, and his reception of the stigmata prior to his death.

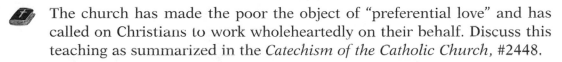 The church has made the poor the object of "preferential love" and has called on Christians to work wholeheartedly on their behalf. Discuss this teaching as summarized in the *Catechism of the Catholic Church*, #2448.

Talk over other sources of conflict between teens and parents, and possible solutions.

Discussion Questions

1. What do you want for your future? What do your parents want for your future?
2. If you found yourself homeless, map out a strategy for surviving the next day, month, and year.
3. Pretend you heard a voice tell you to "build up the church." What would that mean for you?

Project Ideas

Make bird feeders to honor St. Francis. Provide light-weight wood, screening, wood glue, hammers, and nails as needed. The screening should be nailed to the bottom of any design so that bird seed can be placed on it. Encourage the students to paint images of St. Francis on their bird feeders.

Give each participant five small strips of paper, numbered 1 to 5. Ask them to print the names of their five most prized possessions, one on each strip, with their *most* prized possession on strip 1. Have the participants meet with a partner and fan out their strips, blank side showing. Instruct each person to pick one strip from their partner. Then have the two discuss how they would feel if they really lost that possession. Continue in the same way until all the strips have been drawn and discussed.

St. Luke

Session Topics: St. Luke, gospel formation, the early church, Holy Spirit

Icebreaker

Conduct an impromptu talent show. Call on several volunteers to share a secret or known talent. Some sample talents might be wiggling an ear without touching it, singing the *Flintstones* theme song, reciting a poem, standing on one's head or hands for a minute, reciting the Lord's Prayer in another language, or doing ten one-arm pushups. Offer these suggestions and the participants are sure to come up with others. Award a round of applause to all of the volunteers.

Teaching

A *masterpiece* is the greatest work of an artist. It is the product of a large dream and years of toil.

A masterpiece is not limited to works of art. It can be a Grammy-winning CD, an Oscar-winning performance, or a 60-point personal best in a basketball title game.

St. Luke was a member of the early Christian community. He wasn't one of the apostles; in fact, he most likely never met Jesus. Rather, he was a traveling companion of St. Paul and, as Paul described him, a "beloved physician" (Col 4:14). Luke may have been with Paul at the very end of his life (2 Tm 4:11).

The life work or masterpiece for Luke came in the area of writing.

Luke's goal was to write a history of the life of Jesus and an account of the formation of the early church. This was a different approach than the other evangelists took; their concerns were less biographical and more written accounts of the faith.

Luke's finished product was one literary work with two parts. The first part is easy to recognize; it is the gospel of Luke. You may not know that Luke is also the author of the Acts of the Apostles and that Acts is intended to be the second part to Luke's gospel. Both the gospel of Luke and Acts have a common prologue addressing the work to "Theophilus."

As any complete biography would, Luke's includes information about the very beginning of Jesus' life, including the announcement of his birth, his mother's preparations, the birth in a cave, the presentation at the Temple, and another visit to the Temple when Jesus was twelve years old. Most of this information is unique to Luke's gospel.

Luke was a polished writer. He wrote in Greek and his work was for a Gentile, or non-Jewish, audience. An example of this is the way he took great pains to explain Jewish laws that Matthew did not have to explain for his Jewish audience. Also, whereas Matthew took the genealogy from Jesus to Abraham, the father of the Jewish faith, Luke extended it all the way to Adam, the father of the human race.

Luke's gospel (and Acts, as well) is arranged around a journey. Whereas Mark's gospel takes only one chapter to tell of Jesus' travels from Galilee to Jerusalem, Luke's takes ten, from 9:51 to 19:40. During this journey, he introduces many teachings of Jesus, most of them addressed only to the apostles.

The Holy Spirit is also very prominent in Luke. The Spirit is present at Jesus' baptism, leads Jesus to the desert, and returns him to Galilee. When Jesus reads the scroll of the prophet Isaiah in the synagogue, it is the Spirit who identifies him as the Messiah, God's chosen one.

There is no clear information about the end of Luke's life, though early church tradition holds that he wrote his gospel in Greece and died at the age of 84. One thing that is clear is that he was a person who accomplished what he set out to do, the task he outlined in the very first verses of his gospel:

> Many have undertaken to compile a narrative of the events that have been fulfilled among us, just as those who were eyewitnesses from the beginning and ministers of the word have handed them down to us, I too have decided, after investigating everything accurately anew, to write it down in an orderly sequence for you, most excellent Theophilus, so that you may realize the certainty of the teachings you have received (Luke 1:1-4).

Luke's feast day is October 18.

Additional Lessons

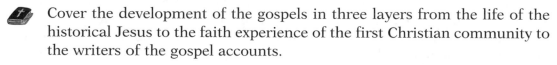

Cover the development of the gospels in three layers from the life of the historical Jesus to the faith experience of the first Christian community to the writers of the gospel accounts.

Read a teaching or parable unique to Luke (e.g., the parable of the lost son in Luke 15). With the participants, discuss how the story you read fits with Luke's overall themes and objectives.

Provide some general biographical background on the other evangelists, including information about their feast days.

Discussion Questions

1. What do you hope will be your life masterpiece?
2. Who are people you feel are excluded from being a part of the church?
3. If you could know one thing about Jesus' hidden years (ages 13 to 30), what would it be?

Project Ideas

Play a Bible quiz game. Give each participant a bible. Ask questions with answers that can be found in Luke or Acts. Divide the group into two teams. Award points to the team that can cite the chapter and verse where the answer can be found.

Ask the participants to imagine that they have been assigned to write a definitive account of Jesus' life. Tell them to each write down the ten most important events from Jesus' life (miracles, teachings, parables, etc.) that would have to go in the story, ranking them in importance from 1 to 10. When they have finished, collect, read, and compare several of the lists.

Halloween/All Saints' Day/All Souls' Day

Session Topics: Halloween, All Saints' Day, All Souls' Day, pagan practices, communion of saints, purgatory

Icebreaker

Give each person a large paper bag and provide several crayons, markers, and scissors. Allow time for everyone to create his or her own mask. When finished, have them put on the masks. Then have a short discussion about some other types of "masks" that adolescents sometimes wear: for example, jock, computer nerd, druggie, gangster, cheerleader. Ask the participants to add more "masks" and tell why they think people their age hide behind some of these behaviors or are labeled in these ways.

Teaching

Until recently Catholic schools were always closed on the holy days of obligation. At Halloween time, this was a great advantage the Catholic school kids had over the public school kids. Because November 1, the Feast of All Saints, was a day off school, Catholic school students always got to stay out late trick-or-treating on Halloween.

Halloween, All Saints' Day, and All Souls' Day (on November 2) are often linked together, though their connections are not as strong as you might imagine.

The name Halloween means "All Hallows (Holy) Eve." Really, the name is a misnomer. Years before Christianity, the Druids marked the start of winter with the burning of the stalks around November 1. Also, it was believed that demons and devils roamed the earth on this night, and the way to ward them off included offering them sweets or disguising oneself in a costume as a demon and roaming with these evil spirits. Parts of these traditions have lasted until today.

All Saints' Day, on the other hand, is a feast established by the church to honor all of the saints in heaven who do not have a special day on one of the other 364 days of the year. These include the many saints who have not been recognized with canonization. Some of your deceased relatives and friends are likely included in those remembered on All Saints' Day.

You might think that the church established this holiday on November 1 as a way to counteract the pagan practices on Halloween. Actually, All Saints' Day was originally held in May. In 844 it was transferred to November 1 so that the many pilgrims who came to Rome to celebrate the day could be fed more easily with the food from the harvest.

All Souls' Day on November 2 was established in the eleventh century. The church has always believed that it should pray for "the souls of the faithfully departed." The tradition around All Souls' Day includes the Catholic belief in purgatory, a condition in which those who have died are "purged" or made clean from their sins in preparation for meeting God in the full joy of heaven. People on earth can aid the souls in purgatory by praying for them, doing works of charity, and offering Masses for the dead. Around the 1500s, priests were permitted to offer three Masses on All Souls' Day for the dead. Today, in your church bulletin, you may see people named, both living and dead, who will have Masses offered for them on a particular day and time.

A tradition in the United States and other countries is for family members to visit and decorate the graves of their deceased family members on All Souls' Day. Also, names of the dead are collected and given to the priest who offers special prayers for them during the month of November.

Today, if you go to a Catholic school, All Saints' Day is probably not a day off. Nevertheless, you may have the chance to celebrate Mass that day with all of your classmates.

Additional Lessons

Read and share the story of St. Stephen, the first Christian martyr, from Acts 6-7.

Present more information on the church's belief in the final purification of the dead, known as purgatory. See the *Catechism of the Catholic Church*, #1030-1032, for more information.

Lead discussion about respect for the dead, including church regulations on the burial of the dead, autopsies, organ donation, and cremation (see *CCC*, #2299-2301).

Discussion Questions

1. What do you imagine will happen to you after you die?

2. Who is someone who has died with whom you feel a special connection? Explain the connection.
3. If there were a blueprint for becoming a saint, what would it include?

Project Ideas

Ask the participants to write and share short biographies (e.g., place and date of birth and death, significant accomplishments) of deceased members of their family who have taken their place with all the saints.

As a group or individual project, have the participants design a costume for a saint (e.g., Carmelite habit for St. Thérèse of Lisieux) that can be worn in a pageant either by them or younger children in their school or religious education program.

The Liturgical Year

Session Topics: the liturgical year, Christ the King, solemnities, feasts, memorials

Icebreaker

Have the participants divide into pairs and designate one person "heads" and the other "tails" before holding a flip-off of eleven coin tosses. The person in the pair whose side appears the most in the eleven flips is the winner of the first round. Have the winners from round one pair up for a second round of seven tosses. Continue eliminating players until one coin toss champion is crowned.

Teaching

If you want to win a friendly wager with a friend, bet that New Year's comes before Christmas.

Well, if you are a Christian who follows the church calendar (also called the liturgical year or Roman calendar), "New Year's" is the Sunday closest to November 30. This is the first Sunday of Advent and the first Sunday of the church year. It is also at least three weeks before Christmas Day!

There is no need for the church to make a new resolution at the start of a new church year. Throughout every year the church celebrates the unfolding story of our salvation told through the events in the life of Jesus Christ.

The most important day of the church year is Easter Sunday, the day Jesus rose from the dead. The other Sundays of the year share in importance; they are sometimes called "little Easters."

The church year is divided into major seasons. Advent is the beginning of the church year. It lasts about four weeks before Christmas, anticipating Jesus' Second Coming and remembering the preparations that took place the first time Christ entered the world as a human being.

141

The Christmas season begins on December 25. In addition to Christmas Day, this season also celebrates the feast of the Holy Family, the Solemnity of the Mother of God, the feast of the Epiphany, and the feast of the baptism of the Lord.

Next, the church enters a period of "ordinary time" in which there is no special theme or focus in the liturgies. Ordinary time ends with Mardi Gras, the day before Ash Wednesday.

Lent is the next major period of the church year. It begins on Ash Wednesday and lasts until Holy Thursday. Lent is a time of doing penance and renewing your baptismal vows. The Easter Triduum ("three days") bridges Lent and the Easter season. It includes the days of Holy Thursday, Good Friday, and Holy Saturday.

Easter is a moveable feast, tied with the Jewish Passover. It is celebrated on the first Sunday after the first full moon of spring. Hence it occurs sometime between March 22 and April 25. The Easter season follows this high holy day, lasting fifty days until Pentecost, the Sunday marking the coming of the Holy Spirit on the church.

Ordinary time resumes after the Easter season and lasts until the end of November. The final day of the church year is the feast of Christ the King. This feast was established by Pope Pius XI in 1925 as a statement against the tide of nations ignoring their Christian roots to follow secular or worldly leaders and ideas. Christians acknowledge only one king, and that is Jesus Christ.

In addition to the Sunday liturgies, the church year includes many other celebrations recalling events from the lives of Jesus, his mother Mary, and great Christian saints. These days are ranked in order of their importance from solemnities, to feasts, to memorials.

A way to tell the change of church seasons is through the difference in colors worn by the priest and used to decorate the altar. You probably know that green is the color for ordinary time. How many of the other liturgical colors can you name? This question might allow for another friendly wager.

Additional Lessons

The feast of Christ the King anticipates the Second Coming of Christ. Present the church's teaching on the creedal statement, "He will come again in glory" (see *Catechism of the Catholic Church*, #668-677).

The establishment of the feast of Christ the King also called for an annual consecration of the world to the Sacred Heart of Jesus. Uncover more of this devotion that originally began in the thirteenth century. Point out the feast of the Sacred Heart of Jesus on the Friday after the second Sunday after Pentecost.

Review the symbolic meaning of the liturgical colors: green (ordinary time), violet (Advent and Lent), white (Easter), and red (Good Friday and feast days).

Discussion Questions

1. What is your favorite season of the church year? Why?
2. What do you think Jesus would be like as a worldly king?
3. White is now the liturgical color worn at funerals, replacing the original black. Why do you think the change was made?

Project Ideas

Give each person a calendar showing all the days of the year. Have them shade in the seasons of the church year with the proper liturgical colors and print the names of as many holy days, saint's days, and other holidays as they know.

Pass out bibles. Have the participants read the parables in Matthew 13 telling what the kingdom of God is like. Then ask them to use these images to help them write or draw their own parable telling what God's kingdom is like. Allow time for the participants to share their ideas with the group.

Thanksgiving

Session Topics: Thanksgiving, feast of Tabernacles, Jesus' healing of the ten lepers

Icebreaker

Print a list of ten scrambled words of people, places, and things associated with Thanksgiving. For example, KTUYER is turkey. Divide the participants into small groups. Give a copy of the list to each small group. Have them work together to unscramble the words. The first group with all the correct answers is the winner. Other possible words to scramble are: cranberry, pilgrim, parade, Thursday, football, pumpkin, stuffing, eucharist, Indian, and family.

Teaching

A stray letter was found at the post office a few years ago causing much worry and concern. The letter, addressed to "Santa Claus, North Pole," was not the problem. The date of the postmark—January 2—led to much discussion.

"Santa never answered the poor child's Christmas letter," one worker worried.

"I hope the little one hasn't lost faith in Santa," said another.

As such letters are, this one was routed to the Chamber of Commerce where a staff was set up to respond. When the letter was opened, everyone in the office was in for quite a surprise. The child, a 6-year-old boy named Edward, had written not to *ask* for gifts but to *thank* Santa for all the presents he received on Christmas day. The staff was heartened by Edward's letter.

Being thankful is a basic human response to all the good God has bestowed on us. St. Paul, for example, closed most of his letters with some expression of thankfulness: "In all circumstances give thanks, for this is the will of God for you in Christ Jesus" (1 Thes 5:18).

Many nations and cultures have reserved special days in the course of a year to offer thanks for God's blessings. The Jewish people have two such festivals, one near the spring harvest (Pentecost) and the other in the fall (Tabernacles or Booths) to offer thanks. In the Middle Ages, a thanksgiving day was held in Germany, France, Holland, and England in conjunction with the feast of St. Martin of Tours on November 11. The day began with Mass and continued with a dance, a parade, and a huge feast highlighted by the serving of wild goose.

When the pilgrims settled in America, they remembered this day of thanksgiving. They decided to have a three-day feast in the autumn of 1621. There was plenty of food available. The native people brought deer. Lobsters, oysters, and fish were also plentiful. But the pilgrims remembered the goose they had once shared in Europe. According to historical accounts, "Governor Bradford sent four men on a fowling so that we might have a more special manner of rejoicing together." The hunting party did find a few geese, but also many turkeys and ducks.

Early in our nation's history, Thanksgiving Day began to be celebrated regularly. During the Civil War, President Abraham Lincoln declared the fourth Thursday in November to be a national holiday. It has been celebrated on that day in the United States in all the years since, except for 1939 and 1940 when President Franklin Roosevelt changed Thanksgiving to the third Thursday to allow for more days of Christmas shopping. Public opinion demanded Thanksgiving be returned to its original day.

Thanksgiving is not a holy day of obligation for Catholics, but many Catholics do attend a special family Mass on that day. Many parishes take up a collection of food products to benefit the poor. Some parishes even sponsor complete Thanksgiving meals for the homeless and homebound.

Usually, the gospel reading for the Thanksgiving Mass is the account, unique to Luke's gospel, of Jesus' healing of the ten Samaritan lepers. After the ten had showed themselves to a priest, as Jesus had instructed, one former leper returned to Jesus, fell at his feet, and thanked him. Jesus' response was: "Where are the other nine?"

We, like the leper and the little boy who received all the Christmas presents, have been gifted abundantly by God. In our church, with the celebration of the eucharist (Greek for "thanksgiving"), every day is a day for thanks. How do you show your thankfulness?

Additional Lessons

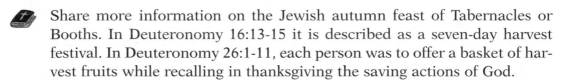

Share more information on the Jewish autumn feast of Tabernacles or Booths. In Deuteronomy 16:13-15 it is described as a seven-day harvest festival. In Deuteronomy 26:1-11, each person was to offer a basket of harvest fruits while recalling in thanksgiving the saving actions of God.

Read and discuss in more detail Jesus' cleansing of the ten lepers (Lk 17:11-19).

Provide information (consider inviting a guest speaker) about an agency in your area that provides daily meals for the homeless. Share relevant details including how many people are served, the number of families present, type of food needed, funding for the agency, etc.

Discussion Questions

1. What is your favorite Thanksgiving Day tradition?
2. When was a time you were surprised by someone who thanked you for something you did?
3. What are you most grateful for?

Project Ideas

Provide stationery and envelopes. Have the participants write a thank-you letter to someone they know: for example, a parent, family member, friend, teacher, neighbor. Arrange for the letters to be delivered.

Prepare several goodwill bags of Thanksgiving items that can be shared with the poor or homebound of your parish or local community. Items to be included in the bag might be canned foods (cranberries, pumpkin pie mix), boxed items (turkey dressing), bread, and apple cider. Donate these goodwill bags as part of a larger parish or civic effort at Thanksgiving.

The Immaculate Conception

Session Topics: the immaculate conception, original sin, dogma, Tradition, Our Lady of Lourdes

Icebreaker

Sketch a large Christmas tree on a piece of newsprint. Have several large Christmas gift catalogs, scissors, glue, and felt-tip markers available. Print the names of the participants on small pieces of paper and put them in a hat. Have each person draw a name, returning the slip if they draw their own. Tell the participants to look through the catalogs for a gift for the person they drew, cut it out, and glue it under the Christmas tree. When all the gifts are under the tree, call the participants one at a time to tell who the gift is for, why they chose it, and to print the person's name on the newsprint above or below the gift.

Teaching

Human beings are born into a sinful condition. This is evident whenever you act in an evil way in spite of your best intentions; envy, greed, and hate may invade your thoughts. Pain, suffering, and death are part of the human experience.

This inherited condition of sin is defined as original sin. The first humans, named Adam and Eve in the Bible, were clothed with God's grace and destined to live forever in eternal happiness. Their personal choice to sin resulted in the state of brokenness we find in ourselves and in the world at large. We are people who are capable of love and goodness, yet also capable of hate and evil.

The church believes that only two people were ever conceived without original sin. One, of course, was Jesus. The other was his mother Mary. On December 8, the church celebrates the feast of the Immaculate Conception to celebrate Mary's clean and pure beginnings from the time she was first conceived. Tradition identifies Mary's parents as St. Anne and St. Joachim, though there is little information on either.

Tradition also plays an important role in the development of this feast. Whereas other Christians look only to the pages of the Bible to name dogma, Catholics believe that God's revelation did not stop some time in the first century when the last pages of the Bible were written. Rather, God continues to reveal himself and the mystery of salvation through the life of living Christians in all generations. This ongoing interpretation and understanding of God's revelation is called Tradition. Catholics believe that the pope and bishops have received the teaching authority of the apostles to interpret and protect the church's Tradition.

The feast of the Immaculate Conception is a good example of how the lived beliefs of the people led to the declaration of a church dogma. From the earliest centuries, written testimony exists that Mary was free from original sin. In the east, this feast was originally called the "Conception of St. Anne," meaning that Anne had conceived Mary. As the centuries went on, devotion to the belief grew, especially among religious orders like the Franciscans and Carmelites. In the fifteenth century, Pope Sixtus IV allowed the whole church to celebrate the Immaculate Conception, but he did not command it. Finally, in 1854, Pope Pius IX elevated the feast to its highest rank when he declared it a dogma of faith that Mary was conceived without original sin. He wrote:

> The most Blessed Virgin Mary was, from the first moment of her conception, by a singular grace and privilege of almighty God and by virtue of the merits of Jesus Christ, Savior of the human race, preserved immune from all stain of original sin (*Ineffablis Deus*).

Interestingly, in the appearances to St. Bernadette at Lourdes, France, in 1858, the Lady eventually identified herself by saying, "I am the Immaculate Conception." Many felt this was Mary giving her approval for the church's recognition of her purity. This belief in the Immaculate Conception of Mary also has roots in the Bible, for the angel Gabriel revealed at the annunciation of Jesus' birth that Mary was "full of grace."

Additional Lessons

Explore more the relationship between Sacred Tradition and Sacred Scripture in transmitting the faith through the ages. See the *Catechism of the Catholic Church*, #80-84.

Point out the relationship between dates the church commemorates in the life of Mary: the Annunciation (March 25) is nine months before Christmas (December 25); the Immaculate Conception (December 8) is celebrated nine months before the birth of Mary (September 8).

Relate the story of Mary's appearances at Lourdes, France, to St. Bernadette. Explain something of how the church officially approves Marian apparitions. Include mention of Our Lady of Guadalupe (feast day on December 12).

Discussion Questions

1. What is a tradition that has been passed on in your family for many generations?
2. If you could find out anything about Mary's childhood, what would you want to know?
3. What would you say to someone who says, "Catholics worship Mary as God?"

Project Ideas

Using a concordance, give the participants every scripture passage that refers to Mary. Ask them to read each passage and to summarize what they know about Mary's life.

Demonstrate how clean water comes from a clean sponge. Point out how it was necessary for the sinless Savior to be born of a mother who was also preserved from sin.

Christmas

Session Topics: Christmas, Christmas season, giving, celebration

Icebreaker

Divide the participants into small groups for a Christmas carol performance. Have them work together to rearrange a carol in a creative way. For example, a group may choose to rewrite the lyrics in a light-hearted way. Or, they may choose to sing the carol in a different style or tempo. Allow a few minutes for preparation. Then have the groups perform the carols for each other.

Teaching

As you enter the teenage years, your feelings for Christmas may be changing. You may no longer sit with the toy advertisements from the Sunday paper and circle all the things you want in the hope that "Santa" will magically enter your house on Christmas morning and give them to you.

At least one adult may have told you, "Christmas is for little children." Where does that leave you?

Certainly there are many basic appealing parts of the holiday that remain. You have a break from school. You may get to see cousins and other family members you only see once a year. And you do get some presents, though maybe not as many as before.

You are definitely at a Christmas crossroads.

Even as you get older, every Christmas should be filled with the magic of the holidays. However, as a teenager, you now have more responsibility in your family, church, and community for making the Christmas spirit come alive. You now need to do for others what has, for most of your life, been done for you.

For example, now you must begin to give as well as receive. Use the days and weeks before Christmas to do some extra chores around the neighborhood to earn money for presents. Then thoughtfully spend some time choosing gifts for your own family members. You'll soon learn the thrill of seeing someone open a present you have chosen and wrapped especially for them.

Give to people outside of your family as well. Do you have grandparents who live nearby? Pay them an extra visit during this month. Volunteer to help them with their own shopping (no charge). If your grandparents live farther away, write them a letter. Send them a copy of your report card (if it is a good one) or a photo of a team you play on. Better yet, record a video Christmas message telling them in your own words how much they mean to you and send it to them.

What can you do for people in your parish and community? Many churches sponsor a "Giving Tree" during Advent. Ornaments are hung on a tree in the church vestibule with descriptions of poor children who will need Christmas gifts. Spend some of your hard-earned money on a toy that you would have loved to have as a young kid but never got. Wrap it carefully. Donate your gift as part of the Giving Tree project or a similar project in your area.

Christmas *is* about giving. At the first Christmas, God the Son, the Second Person of the Trinity, gave his life to the world by becoming a human being. God himself came to the world in the person of Jesus to bring salvation. Eventually, Jesus would be rejected and put to death, but he would be accepted by the millions and millions of Christians who lived then and in the years since.

Let's end this short lesson on Christmas with a couple of often repeated phrases. *Christmas is the best time of the year*. You can always keep it so as long as you keep *Christ in Christmas!*

Additional Lessons

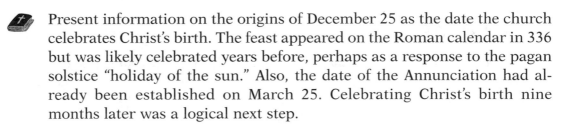

Present information on the origins of December 25 as the date the church celebrates Christ's birth. The feast appeared on the Roman calendar in 336 but was likely celebrated years before, perhaps as a response to the pagan solstice "holiday of the sun." Also, the date of the Annunciation had already been established on March 25. Celebrating Christ's birth nine months later was a logical next step.

Define the term "Incarnation" and present the church's teaching on this mystery. See the *Catechism of the Catholic Church*, #461-463.

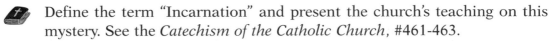

Read and compare the infancy narratives in Matthew 1-2 and Luke 2.

Discussion Questions

1. How have your own feelings about Christmas changed from the time you were a young kid?
2. What are some of your family traditions on Christmas Day? For example, when do you open presents? When do you go to Mass? Where do you eat dinner?

3. What is the best Christmas gift you ever gave to someone?

Project Ideas

Establish or participate in a Giving Tree project as described above. During the time the teens are together, have them wrap and organize the presents that have been collected.

Have the participants surprise younger children in the parish school or religious education program by decorating their classroom while they are away. One possibility is to leave a decorated Christmas tree in the classroom with a note from Santa to each of the children by name.

December

The Holy Innocents

Session Topics: the holy innocents, Herod, justice

Icebreaker

Print the names of celebrities (sports, television, movies, music) familiar to teens on adhesive slips of paper. The celebrities can be living or dead. You can even choose cartoon characters. Have one slip for each person. Have the group stand in a large circle. Tell them you are going to put the adhesive slips on their backs. When everyone has one, they are to mingle around the room and ask "yes or no" questions (e.g., "Am I a musician?" or "Am I on a television commercial?") of one another until they determine the name of their celebrity. Tell them they can ask each person only one question. Play until everyone has guessed his or her celebrity.

Teaching

How sad it is when an innocent person is punished. You may know the feeling. Have you ever been in a class where all the students had to stay after school because one or two kids did something wrong? Or, have you been on a team when you had to run an extra lap because of the mistake of another?

When you were in about third or fourth grade, the injustice of such punishments likely drove you nuts. Eight- and nine-year-olds are developmentally conditioned to accept only a black and white distribution of justice. Any other way merits a cry of "Not fair!"

These days you are probably more aware that life is not always fair. Maybe you lost the science fair to the classmate whose parents did all the work, or you are the only one in your class not allowed to go to the Friday night football game without an adult chaperone. Not fair, maybe, but it's just the way it is.

There are often times when the truly innocent are severely punished. The feast of the Holy Innocents on December 28 remembers one of those times.

157

King Herod was one of the cruelest rulers in all of history. During his reign from 37 to 4 B.C. Herod had executed anyone he deemed a threat to his rule. He drowned his brother-in-law. A few years before the birth of Christ, Herod had two of his own sons and nearly three hundred court officials who sided with them killed.

As Matthew's gospel reports, Herod felt endangered by the report of a newborn king of the Jews. He sent three magi as spies to Bethlehem to get information about Jesus. When the magi never returned and Herod realized he had been deceived, he became furious and "ordered the massacre of all the boys in Bethlehem and its vicinity two years old and under" (Mt 2:16).

Who knows how many children were actually murdered? Given that Bethlehem was a small village of about 2,000 people, there were likely at least thirty boys of that age who were murdered.

These innocent children were the first to give their lives for Christ, and from its earliest days, the church remembered them with their own feast.

Today, there are many other innocent children who are remembered in prayer: the uncared for, unloved, and starving children who continue to populate the world. And, thousands and thousands of unborn children are tragically aborted each year.

The next time you are forced to accept a punishment for something you did not do, offer it in memory of other innocents who are forced to endure and offer much more, including their lives.

Additional Lessons

Investigate how the feast of the Holy Innocents is related to the feast of the Boy Bishop, originally celebrated on December 28 but later moved to the eve of St. Nicholas Day on December 5. (In honor of St. Gregory, the patron saint of students and choirboys, young boys would dress as bishops and preach a sermon at a devotional service. Later, adults took this role, often dressing as St. Nicholas and distributing candy and gifts.)

Present something of contemporary church teaching on *limbo*, that is, the destiny of the souls of the unbaptized. A Vatican II understanding of limbo is that God extends mercy and love universally and destines all people for heaven.

Offer up-to-date statistics on the number of abortions performed in your country in the past year.

Discussion Questions

1. Tell about a time you were punished for something you didn't do.
2. What is one atrocity against justice that you are aware of in your local community, nation, or world today?
3. What does it mean to you to be fair?

Project Ideas

Have the participants work in small groups to prepare and enact role-plays of common situations in which people their own age are punished for things they did not do.

Arrange for the participants to clean, repair, paint, or otherwise refurbish the parish nursery or crying room. Possible related activities: painting, sorting toys and books, repairing broken toys, or going door-to-door soliciting other children's items that can be used in the nursery.

Part II

Sunday Fun Throughout the Year
Four Seasons of Activities

Christmas Shopping at the Mall

What's Needed:

☞ money for Christmas presents and food
☞ a Christmas list

Description:

The mall may not be a fun place for teens to go with their parents, but they absolutely love it when they can go with one another.

Reserve a Sunday in December for some last-minute Christmas shopping. Have the participants bring their Christmas savings (it doesn't have to be a lot) and Christmas gift list with them to the mall.

Treat this adventure as you would a trip to an amusement park. Make them stay together in groups of two or three. Bigger groups of traveling kids, even if they are paying customers, are not usually appreciated by the merchants.

Reserve a few tables in the mall's food court and give the teens a designated time to return. When everyone is back, have them promise secrecy to one another and show some of the gifts they bought for friends and family.

Finally, enjoy a food court meal or snack together.

Christmas Caroling

What's Needed:

☞ addresses of homebound parishioners
☞ one Christmas card for each person or family you will visit
☞ one song sheet with the lyrics for Christmas carols for each participant
☞ hot chocolate, cookies, or other Christmas snack treats

Description:

Work with the pastoral minister in charge of visits to the homebound to arrange for the teens to sing Christmas carols at their homes. Make sure to set a two-hour window of time when the teens will come to their homes to sing.

Before leaving the parish, practice the songs with the teens. Remind them to leave their "coolness" behind and really belt out the songs, as those they visit will really appreciate the effort. Also, have each teen sign Christmas cards for the people they will visit.

Try to visit at least six to eight different homes. (You will need parent drivers to transport teens if the homes are well out of the area.)

When the group has finished its tour, return to the parish for some hot chocolate, cookies, and other Christmas snacks.

Free Baby-Sitting for Christmas Shoppers

What's Needed:

☞ a nursery or other suitable room to hold teens and younger children
☞ craft supplies for a Christmas project
☞ VCR, television, and several children's videos
☞ board games and toys to keep children busy
☞ snacks and drinks

Description:

Offer a three-hour baby-sitting service for parents who need to do last-minute Christmas shopping. The teens baby-sit the children at the parish while the parents are shopping. (Recommendation: Do not accept children who have not been potty-trained.) Plan this event a couple of weekends before Christmas, with heavy publicity in the church bulletin.

Arrange several stations where the teens can interact and supervise the children, for example, two or three different craft areas where teens lead the construction of things like Christmas wreaths, coloring projects, or the cutting out of snowflakes from white construction paper. At another station, keep several videos on hand. It's preferable to have short thirty-minutes videos rather than full-length pictures in order to continually attract the attention of more and more kids. Finally, many teens can spend one-on-one time with children playing board games and interacting in many other forms of play.

Make sure to provide permission slips and sign-in sheets as needed. Keep the teens around to clean up the nursery area when the baby-sitting time is over.

Super Bowl Party

What's Needed:

☞ ping pong table and/or billiards table
☞ several board games like Parcheesi, Trivial Pursuit, Clue, checkers, and chess
☞ lots of chips, dip, sodas, and other "tailgate" food
☞ at least one mini-van or similar car with a hatchback
☞ a large television to watch the game

Description:

Hold this event on Super Bowl Sunday, usually the last Sunday of January. Plan it as if your group were actually tailgating outside the stadium before the big game.

Start the festivities about one hour before kick-off. If possible, back the mini-van up to the entrance of the room you have reserved and put the snack items in the back of the hatchback. Have a television turned on to the pre-game show to maintain a football mood. Have plenty of indoor games like ping pong, billiards, and board games available for the participants to pass the pre-game time.

Before the game, allow the participants to guess on several trivia and game-related items that are bound to occur. Award prizes to the person who wins each category, for example:

- elapsed time of national anthem
- commercial appearing first after the kickoff
- which team wins the coin toss
- which player scores the first touchdown
- city where the blimp originates
- total score after the first quarter
- player catching the first pass

Plan to complete all of the events by half-time, but allow teens to stay for the entire game.

Team Bowling

What's Needed:

☞   old T-shirts
☞   markers or paints to decorate the T-shirts
☞   cash to rent the lanes

Description:

Take sign-ups for this event and arrange for enough lanes so that four people can bowl on each lane. Before you go, divide the students into groups of four based on bowling abilities. Have the students rank themselves as excellent, good, fair, or beginner. Try to make sure each group has one of each type of bowler. Tell the groups to agree on a team name and then to decorate their "bowling T-shirts" accordingly, including individual nicknames. Have them wear the shirts to the lanes.

Play a round robin, double-elimination tournament that takes the total score of each team per game to determine winners. Continue until there is a champion.

Cross for Life

What's Needed:

☞ large posterboard
☞ dark markers or paint

Description:

January has become a time to remember the many lives of unborn children lost to abortion. A January 1973 Supreme Court decision, Roe v. Wade, ruled that abortions were legal in the United States.

Many right-to-life groups sponsor a public prayer for life in January. One way you can participate is to have the teens make posters proclaiming their support for life, for example, "Choose Life," "Teens for Life," "Abortion Stops a Beating Heart," or "Pray to End Abortion." The slogans or the event do not have to be politically charged, but simply an expression by the teens of support for all life.

Seek permission from the city government for the teens to form a human cross on the sidewalks at the intersection of a well-traveled street in your community. Have them hold up their signs as motorists pass by.

This is a good event for parents and other adults to join in. It can elicit both pre- and post-event conversation on this crucial issue and the expectations Christ and the church have for all people to stand up for life.

Downhill Action

What's Needed:

☞ a place for downhill skiing, sledding, snow boarding, or ice block racing
☞ the equipment and money necessary for the activity that is chosen
☞ waterproof clothing for the teens

Description:

Believe it or not, this event is suitable even for places without snow. However, teens do love to go skiing, sledding, or snow boarding, so if it is at all possible, arrange for a day trip to a local ski resort where the more experienced skiers can take to the slopes, while the newcomers can take a lesson and work the bunny hills.

Other downhill possibilities which might cost less are sledding and snow boarding. Plan the event in conjunction with a recent snowstorm and at a nearby hill.

If you live in an area without snow, ice block racing provides many of the same thrills. All you need are several large blocks of ice and a grassy hill that is preferably moist with rain or dew. The teens take turns sitting on the ice blocks, getting a head-start push, and sliding to the bottom of the hill. This really works and is a lot of fun.

Golf courses are great places for ice block racing, providing you get the permission of the proprietor.

Valentine Photo-Op

What's Needed:

☞ one Polaroid camera for every four students
☞ color film for the cameras
☞ prizes for the winners

Description:

Have the students work in groups of four (with one high school student or adult leader) to canvass the immediate neighborhood (give some boundaries) for the following photo opportunities with these Valentine themes:

* Near a Valentine card display
* Holding a candy Valentine
* With a married couple (ask how long they have been married)
* At a romantic location
* With three of you forming a human valentine
* Near a sign advertising a Valentine dance, special sale, or other social occasion
* With someone wearing lots of red
* With a fancy engagement ring

Rule:

Trade off taking the photos. Everyone in the group except the person taking the picture should be visible in the photo.

When the group returns, award prizes to the photos based on creativity and quality on a scale of 1 to 3. Give prizes to winners for each photo or to one overall winner.

Indoor Gym Games

What's Needed:

☞ a gym or auditorium with a large open floor space
☞ two brooms, a large cloth ball, a round Nerf ball, a plastic ball, plastic bat, and any items needed for other games you choose

Description:

A day of gym games is perfect for the colder winter months. Here are three unusual games your group can play besides the traditional basketball and volleyball.

Broom Hockey. Divide the participants into two groups, each standing on opposite long sides of the court. Put the cloth ball and the two brooms in the center of the court. Give each person on both teams a number as listed below. Explain that when you call a person's number he or she is to run to the center, grab a broom, and try to "sweep" the ball to the wall under his or her team's basket (designate which end wall belongs to each team). Keep calling numbers until everyone gets a turn. (This game also works in traditional basketball. When you call a number the two combatants run for the ball and then play each other in a full-court one-on-one game.)

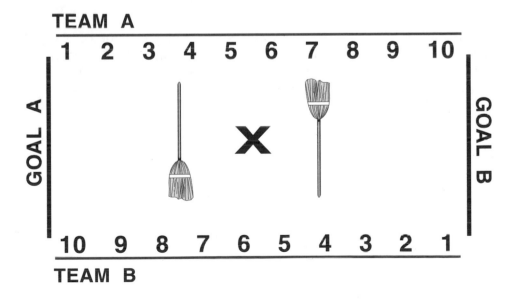

Target Practice. Number and position the teams as in broom hockey. This time place a round Nerf ball in the center of the circle. When you call a number the person who gets to it first picks up the ball and tries to throw it at the wall behind the opposing team. Anyone on the opposing team may block the ball to keep it from hitting the wall. Then, they pass the ball to their team representative, who is still in the center, who tries to throw and hit the other wall. The first player to hit the wall wins a point for his or her team.

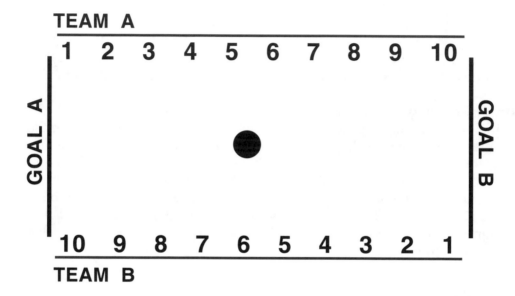

Hit Ball. Mark out bases, divide up teams, and play a game of baseball with the plastic ball and plastic bat. The only major rule change from regular baseball is that the players can throw and hit the runner with the ball to get an out. However, throwing at the head is not permitted.

Spring Dance

What's Needed:

☞ DJ with sound system and plenty of CDs or other suitable arrangements for dancing music

☞ arrangements made to invite junior high teens from other church youth groups to the dance

Description:

Junior high teens *will* dance and *are* able to behave appropriately at a dance given the right combination of freedom and supervision.

Spring is a good time to hold the dance because the boys and girls have now established better relationships than they may have had at the beginning of the year. Hold the dance in the evening, either after a Saturday night Mass or on a Sunday before a day off from school. Make every effort to include other teens from neighboring church youth groups. Not only is this a great way to collaborate, but having more people at a dance makes for much more fun. Here are some other recommendations:

- Hold the dance in a large auditorium, gym, or parish hall.
- Darken the room by turning off most or all of the main lighting. However, add an appropriate amount of lighting with strobe lights, black lights, spotlights, etc.
- Require semi-formal dress. Teens are less likely to goof around when they are dressed up.
- Have the teens help pre-select the music that will be used, or check with the DJ to make sure he or she has all the music teens like.
- Invite parents to chaperone. However, don't oversaturate the area with adults. Try to invite parents of teens with high self-confidence who will not be bothered by their parents' presence.
- Invite several respected high school teens, both boys and girls. Sometimes these older teens can lead off the dancing in order to encourage everyone else to join in.
- Charge admission to the dance. This will either defray the cost of the DJ or provide for a good fund-raiser.
- Supervise the bathrooms. Call the parents of anyone who seriously misbehaves.

Gym Rats

What's Needed:

☞ an indoor or outdoor basketball court
☞ a supply of basketballs

Description:

The basketball court lends itself to a number of variations of basketball that are suitable for large or small gatherings of both boys and girls. One way to involve the largest number of players is to play two simultaneous games of five-on-five half-court basketball. Prior to the start of the game, give each team slips of paper marked 1 to 5. Tell them to decide on their team's "best" player and give the person slip 1. Then have them rank the other players 2 to 5. When this is done, surprise the teams by telling them that the person holding the "5" will get 5 points whenever he or she makes a basket, the "4" person will receive 4 points, and so on. Have them start the game, playing to a designated score (e.g., 20). Rotate all the teams in a round robin tournament.

Other basketball games:

Lay-up Relay. This is like a regular relay race. Players from two teams race to opposite baskets, shoot a lay-up, and return to give the ball to the next player. Limit the number of shots each player takes to 3.

Free-throw Contest. Pair up the participants, matching the better players with beginners. Hold a "best of 20" free-throw contest with each player on a team shooting ten free throws. Compare the scores of each team to determine a winner.

Stationary Basketball. Hold a round robin two-on-two tournament. The only difference from a usual game is that only one player on each team can shoot the ball and that player must remain stationary in any one spot on the half court. The stationary players can pick their own spots. The other players work hard to dribble, rebound, and pass the ball to their teammates.

Team Around the World. This is a game where the winning team must make a series of shots all the way around the basketball key. Players on each team alternate taking shots as their team's turn comes up at each spot.

What's High School All About?

What's Needed:

☞ a panel made up of high school students from the parish who attend the high school(s) most of the junior high group will eventually attend

Description:

This event is designed to orient the junior high teens to the next step in their education: high school.

Invite at least three or four high school students from the parish to form a panel and share with the younger teens some basic information on what to expect when they go to high school. Plan to prep the high school students so that they can talk on subjects like the following:

- academics (difficult classes, how much homework to expect, grading scale, types of tests, favorite teachers, etc.)
- extracurricular activities (sports, band, cheerleading, drama, student government, newspaper, yearbook, other clubs, etc.)
- social (how freshmen are treated by upperclassmen, the preponderance of drugs and alcohol, how high school students spend weekends, dating etiquette, dances, etc.)

Allow plenty of opportunity for the junior high students to dialogue and ask questions of the high school panel.

You may wish to combine the panel discussion with a drama, music, or athletic event that is taking place at the high school. Arrange for the junior high students to attend the event either before or after the panel discussion.

Inter-Youth Group Social

What's Needed:

☞ arrangements made to cosponsor an event with a youth minister and youth group from another church

☞ video camera, videotape, VCR, television, and/or other items needed for any events you choose

☞ plenty of refreshments

Description:

Arrange with a youth minister from another church to bring your two groups together for one common event. This is a concrete way for teens to learn that the church goes well beyond the bounds of their own families and neighborhoods.

Prior to the day the groups come together, prepare by having the teens from the two groups exchange letters telling about themselves, their school, their parish, and their families.

As a group project, have your teens work on making a video that gives some background on themselves and some insight into their lives. This video may be themed after the reality programs like MTV's *Real World* or in any other style your teens decide on.

Welcome the teens to your parish with plenty of hospitality. If possible, include them in the full day of programming, including Mass and the lesson. Plan to use an icebreaker that allows the teens from the different groups to become familiar with their names (for example, see page 117).

Have your teens show the video they produced. Then ask members of the other youth group to tell about their church and group, how it seems similar and different from your own.

Finally, allow the teens to join in some shared fun, for example, a volleyball game, bowling, miniature golf, or simply listening to music and sharing food.

Easter Egg Hunt

What's Needed:

☞ many wrapped Easter candies
☞ paper bags in which the children can put their candy
☞ a few special plastic eggs indicating the reception of special prizes
☞ special prizes (stuffed animal, larger piece of candy, etc.)
☞ a large outdoor space to hold the Easter egg hunt
☞ an alternate indoor space in case of rain

Description:

Have the junior high participants sponsor an Easter egg hunt for the younger children in the parish. This can be held on Easter Sunday or on one of the other Sundays of the Easter season.

Arrange for a large outdoor space (preferably a grassy area) where the teens can hide wrapped candy. Also have them hide a few special plastic eggs with notes indicating that the person who finds it wins a special prize.

Divide the children into two or three groups by age; for example, preschoolers, K/1, and 2/3. Give the younger groups a head start at collecting some candies, or hold completely separate hunts.

Have the teens organize the advertising details of the event, help young children find eggs, distribute prizes, and arrange for the cleanup.

To extend the afternoon, you may wish to have the teens plan and perform for the younger children a short Easter play that depicts in some way the good news of Jesus' resurrection.

Awards Banquet

What's Needed:

☞ a copy of the bingo card described below for each participant
☞ award ribbons with attached blank cards
☞ slips of paper with each person's name and a bowl to put them in
☞ pens, markers, and crayons
☞ arrangements for a "fancy" meal to accompany the awards banquet

Description:

This is an event that works well after the teens have spent some time together and have become fairly well acquainted.

To begin, have the group play a game of "People Bingo." Prepare a bingo card with at least 16 squares. Print a "talent" or "skill" in each square that the teens might be able to share or demonstrate, for example:

- recite a poem
- do a fifteen-second handstand
- sing the "Brady Bunch" theme song
- French braid hair
- introduce himself/herself in a language besides English
- know the name of last season's Heisman Trophy winner
- tell a (clean) joke

Give each person a bingo card prepared with items like those listed above. Tell them to get one signature for every square. A person can only sign another person's card one time. A signature on a particular square indicates that a person has that talent.

Play until a person yells "bingo." To check if he or she is the winner, randomly call on some of the people who signed the card and ask them to demonstrate their skills. If all checks out, the person holding the card is the winner. If not, continue playing the game until someone else has bingo.

After the game, pass out award ribbons with attached blank cards to each person. Have them draw a slip of paper with the name of a person in the group (not their own name). Then have them create a positive award for the person whose name they drew and write it on the card with the ribbon. The award should be related to the person's personality, contribution to the group, or talents (e.g., "Most Energetic" or "Best Knowledge of Sports").

Arrange for a fancier-than-normal meal. (It may be "catered" by parents, or you may wish to have the group eat at a restaurant.) Around the meal table, call on each person to explain the award he or she is giving and then give it to the person.

Visit With Older Adults

What's Needed:

☞ homebound parishioners willing to accept teenage visitors, or arrangements made with board and care facility to visit its residents

☞ transportation to the places the teens will be visiting

Description:

Sunday is typically a time to visit with family, especially grandparents and other older relatives. Expand on this practice by having the teens visit homebound parishioners or residents of a nearby board and care facility.

Arrange the visits well ahead of time with the parish minister who is responsible for visiting the homebound and/or bringing the eucharist to these parishioners. Limit the home visits to a maximum of four teens at each home. The visit should be a combination of talking and listening done by the teens and their hosts. Subjects the teens should be prepared to talk about include:

- names and basic family information (parents' names and occupations, number of brothers and sisters, home address)
- school grade and favorite and worst subjects
- extracurricular interests (sports, music, drama)
- description of religious education program

The teens should ask the older person questions as well, for example:
- How long have you lived in the parish?
- What memories do you have of your teenage years?
- How was the church different when you were growing up than it is now?
- What are some things you enjoy doing now?

If home visits are impractical, have the entire group of teens visit a board and care facility. Residents gathered in a common area always enjoy hearing teens sing a song. A song is a great way to break the ice. Then, send the teens in groups of two or three to visit individual residents. Follow the same dialoguing procedures as above.

Spring Cleaning

What's Needed:

☞ plenty of plastic trash bags
☞ work gloves for each participant
☞ cleaning items, rakes, or other tools based on the nature of the project

Description:

Volunteer the group to help clean up a public area in your community. Clean up means bagging trash and collecting larger discards like old tires. Make sure that recyclables like aluminum cans are separated from the rest of the trash.

Possible areas to hold the project: along a river bank, in a wooded area, on a beach, in a park, at a vacant lot.

A variation of this project is to divide the teens into smaller groups of four or five and have them do spring cleaning (leaf raking, painting, sweeping) at the homes of elderly parishioners or around the parish grounds.

Big Amusement Park Trip

What's Needed:

☞ transportation
☞ adult chaperones
☞ money for admission to the park

Description:

This event is one of the stalwarts of your program. Most junior high age teens look forward to a trip to an amusement park such as Six Flags. (Six Flags advertises that they are within a one-day drive for everyone in the country. Check out what is available in your area if you don't already know.)

Some recommendations for the trip:

• Attend Mass and do the lessons and activities on Saturday evening. Begin the amusement park trip on Sunday morning.
• Require all of the teens in your group to invite someone to attend the trip *and* Mass who does not regularly attend church.
• Reserve a bus to transport the teens and chaperones. Include the cost of the bus in the entire package.
• Arrange a group rate for admission tickets from the park.
• It is usually okay to allow the teens to enjoy the amusement park without adults in their groups. However, make sure at least four teens are in one group. Also, have several check-in points throughout your time at the park. Keep a phone beeper with you so that the teens can reach you in case of an emergency.
• Keep a list of the teens' phone numbers with you so that you can reach their parents in case any problems arise.

Plan to stop at a fast-food restaurant on the way back. During this time you can personally meet the guests the teens have brought on the trip and invite them back to a future event you are planning.

5K In-Line Skating

What's Needed:

☞ in-line skates, helmets, and pads for every participant
☞ a safe 5K (3.1 mile) course laid out in the nearby vicinity and maps of the course for every participant
☞ race "officials" stationed at various points throughout the course
☞ numbers printed on paper and safety pins for all the racers
☞ a stopwatch

Description:

You can make the 5K in-line skating event as competitive as you wish, but be sure to open the event to both the "serious racers" and the "Sunday cruisers."

Set out a 3.1 mile course on relatively quiet neighborhood streets. If possible, include a stretch through a park where in-line skating is permitted. Station adult volunteers along the course to keep track of the participants and to remind them to skate safely. Give each skater a number. Ask the more experienced skaters to start near the front of the pack, the less experienced skaters near the rear.

Start timing the racers at the beginning of the race. As they finish, record their times. Keep the score sheet so that you can begin to keep course records. Award prizes at your discretion.

If your group is really adventurous they may want to attempt a 10K race!

Miniature Golf

What's Needed:

☞ money for admission for 18 holes of miniature golf
☞ transportation to the miniature golf course
☞ several small prizes to award to the teens (e.g., candy, ribbons, etc.)

Description:

A trip to the local miniature golf course remains a popular outing for teens. Call the local miniature golf course and inquire about a group discount.

Once at the course, divide the teens into foursomes and let them begin playing. Tell them you will be offering a few special prizes at the end of eighteen holes, but don't tell them for what. Remind them to write down their scores.

As the foursomes return, collect their scorecards. Award several prizes for things like:

• low score on hole 7
• most holes in one
• low team (foursome) score
• low individual score
• high score on hole 11
• high team score
• high individual score

Some courses offer a discount on replays. You may want to have the group go through again just for fun!

Swim Party/Inner Tube Water Polo

What's Needed:

☞ a recreation center or house with a pool
☞ hot dogs, chips, drinks for a cookout
☞ several large rubber inner tubes or similar flotation devices
☞ a plastic ball (basketball size)
☞ two lounge chairs set up as goals

Description:

Summer is the time for a pool party. Check with local schools or recreation centers to find out how you might go about reserving a pool for your group. Or, inquire in the parish if someone with a pool might be willing to sponsor such an event. Include a cookout as part of the festivities. Divide the cost of the event among the teens.

Mostly the teens will be able to entertain themselves with swimming, eating, and playing regular pool games like "Marco Polo." If there is a diving board, you may suggest that they toss the plastic ball to a person jumping, diving, or flipping off. They can enjoy watching for the most acrobatic catches.

Inner tube water polo is played by setting up two lounge chairs on their sides at opposite ends of the pool (on the pavement, not in the water). Divide the group into two teams, with each person sitting in an inner tube against the wall near their own goal. Say "go" and throw the plastic ball to the middle of the pool. Players from both teams paddle to the ball. The team that retrieves it begins its assault on the other goal. A point is awarded for any ball that hits on the seat part of the chair, but the player has to have thrown the ball from the inner tube. You can permit lots of rough stuff as long as the players remain in their inner tubes at all times.

If there are not enough inner tubes to go around, adapt with other kinds of floating devices.

Tennis Court Action

What's Needed:

☞ some reserved tennis courts for your entire group
☞ tennis rackets for every participant
☞ posterboard and marker
☞ a good supply of tennis balls
☞ a volleyball or four-square ball

Description:

Being out on the tennis court makes for enjoyable summer fun, especially later in the day or earlier in the morning when the weather is cooler. If possible, arrange for a tennis coach or experienced player (e.g., a player on the high school team) to give the teens a basic tennis lesson on how to hold the racket, the various strokes, how to serve, how to keep score, etc.

Then set up two or three divisions of novice, intermediate, and experienced players to compete in a round robin singles tournament. Keep track of the tournament results on a posted chart.

Or, hold a doubles tournament. Pair experienced and inexperienced players on the same teams. Again, keep results and play until a champion is crowned.

Finally, as an interlude, play a game using the rules of tennis with a volleyball. Allow three or four players on each team. Remind the players to be aware of the spiking!

Water Slide

What's Needed:

☞ swimsuits and towels
☞ transportation
☞ money for admission

Description:

Enormous water slides at lakes, beaches, and campgrounds have become common across the nation. There is likely such a place in your area.

Plan this trip for a hot summer Sunday. Check with the water park to find out if it has a group discount rate. Also inquire about different rates available for non-peak hours—sometimes these parks will discount admissions late in the evening.

As you would with an amusement park trip, require the teens to stay in groups of at least two or three. Designate certain meeting times and places when you expect them to check in with you or another adult. You may wish to arrange for your entire group to line up together for either the first or last slide ride of the day. This will allow everyone to enjoy being together as a group at least once during the day.

Good Old-Fashioned Cookout

What's Needed:

☞ cookout food (burgers, hot dogs, chips, sodas, cake)
☞ grills, charcoal, matches
☞ items for games (see below)

Description:

This event works well for groups just getting acquainted. Reserve a place at a local park with cookout grills or at any place with a large open field.

Keep the food cooking and available throughout the event so that the teens can eat whenever they want during the activities. Here are standard games that always seem to work well in groups with both boys and girls:

Softball. This is a game the entire group can play. If you don't want to require the teens to bring gloves, play with a larger, spongier ball so that they will be able to catch it with their hands. Old towels work just fine for bases.

Capture the Flag. This remains a popular game, especially when it is played in a large open space. Divide the area into two sides. Put the flags (towels) toward the rear of each side. One goalie for each team is permitted to guard the flag. Also reserve a jail on each side. This is the area for captured opponents. The object of the game is to retrieve the opposing team's flag without being touched. Those who are touched are sent to the opposing team's jail. The teens can fill you in on the other details.

Frisbee Football. This is played like regular football as teams move toward their opposing team's end zone. In this game, a Frisbee is used instead of a football. One team starts with the "ball" at its own twenty yard line. Teammates pass from one teammate to another all the way down the field. There is no running after a catch and opponents have to back at least three feet off the passer.

Steal the Balloon. Remember the game "steal the bacon"? This game is similar except a water balloon is placed in the middle of a circle of participants. Give each person a number. When you call two numbers, those players race to the center of the circle for the balloon. The person who gets there first is allowed to douse the opponent before he or she gets back to the circle. Toward the end of the afternoon, a plain old water balloon fight would be great.

Pay and Play Olympics

What's Needed:

☞ a large football field with at least one goal post
☞ softball, 6 hula hoops, several cones, plastic baseball, plastic baseball bat, four-square ball, and other items for any other games you choose
☞ 25 cents per teen per event
☞ a scorekeeper for each event

Description:

In "Pay and Play Olympics" the teens pay a quarter to participate in each field event. Scores are recorded for each person at each event. At the end of the competition, a percentage of the event profits (e.g., $1) is given to the person with the winning score. Listed below are some events you can include for this outdoor event. Feel free to add some others!

Obstacle Course. Mark an obstacle course with cones around the football field and surrounding area. The course may include running up bleachers, climbing over a low fence, navigating a path through bushes or woods, as well as running on the field. Record the times for each participant.

Softball Throw. Set up six hula hoops in three rows of 3, 2, and 1 in pyramid form on the 50 yard line. Have the participants remain behind a line (e.g., 20 yard line for stronger throwers, 35 yard line for weaker throwers) and throw a softball aiming for the hula hoops. Allow three throws per quarter. Award points as following for each throw:

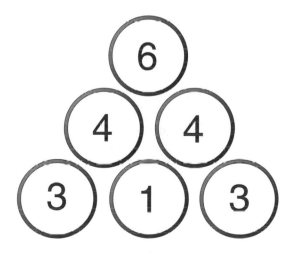

Home Run Derby. Use cones to set up three "home run lines" with a graduating value of points as below:

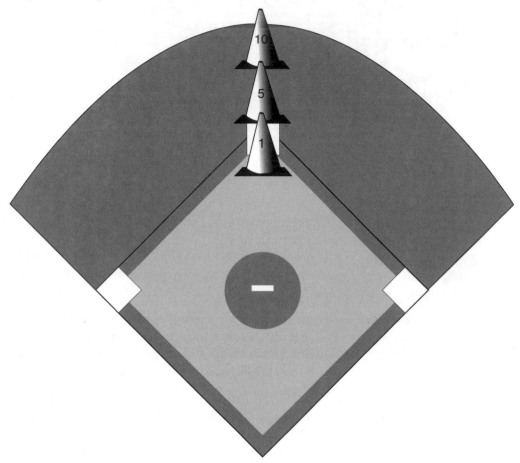

Give each batter five swings for a quarter. A fly ball landing in one of the sections gives that number of points. Total all of the points for five rounds to give the person a score.

Rubber Ball Field Goal Contest. Using a rubber dodge ball, have the participants attempt field goals through the football uprights. Allow them three kicks per quarter and to choose the yard line from which they will attempt the kick. The only rule is that the ball must be kicked from ground (no punts). Record the yard line of the farthest successful kick for each person.

Garage Concert

What's Needed:

☞ a teenage band willing to play a free concert for your group (If such a group is not available, you can substitute with an excellent CD player, large speakers, and plenty of appropriate CDs.)

☞ refreshments for the musicians and the audience

Description:

The history of rock 'n' roll is filled with stories of famous groups who formed as teenagers, wrote music together, and rehearsed their music in the garage of one of their members.

Seek out a band of high school musicians from your parish who would be willing to perform an impromptu concert/rehearsal for your group. (It would be all the better if the musicians played a version of Christian rock. If you are unsuccessful in locating a band through your own parish, call the youth minister of a nearby church for recommendations.)

Once arranged, have the teens meet where the group rehearses (a garage!) or, if possible, invite them to play at the parish. Between songs, interview the band members about their talents, dreams, and aspirations regarding their music. Serve some refreshments at the end of the concert.

Dinner on Wheels

What's Needed:

☞ any kind of transportation other than cars (e.g., in-line skates or bikes)
☞ approximately $5 to $10 for the complete meal (the teens will need their own money)

Description:

This is a progressive meal in which the teens travel by in-line skates or bikes to several different restaurants in the area. Divide the meal into at least four courses. Start out with something healthy like a salad or fruit at a health store or coffee shop. Next, move to a bakery for a slice of fresh bread. (Send one person into the bakery without skates to buy the bread and bring it outside. Have the group sit on a curb or nearby bench to eat the bread.) Then, move to a popular pizza place for the main course: pizza pies. Finally, have dessert at a local yogurt or ice cream store.

To add meaning to the event, begin each part of the meal with a blessing over the food and an appropriate scripture reading of your choice.

Bean Ball Tournament

What's Needed:

☞ a gym or auditorium with a large open floor space, preferably marked for a full basketball court
☞ three rubber four-square balls (preferably slightly deflated)

Description:

This game is an interesting version of dodge ball in which boys and girls play together, and often the person with the weakest arm is the last one remaining.

Divide the participants into two even teams of both boys and girls. Send each team against opposite walls underneath the baskets. Place the three four-square balls an equal distance apart from one another on the half-court line.

When you say "go" the teams will race to take the balls back to their side. Anyone who gets one of the balls has to retouch the starting back wall before he or she can throw the ball and get someone out.

Once the walls have been retouched by those with the balls, a game like dodge ball is under way. However, those holding a ball can throw only in the area from the hash mark on their side of the court to the half court line (see diagram on the next page). Make sure to emphasize this rule. If a person throws from behind the hash mark, he or she is out for the game.

Other ways to get out of the game:

• a person is hit by a ball on the fly (anywhere on the body, including the head)
• a person from one team crosses over the half court line
• a person throws the ball and it is caught on the fly by someone on the other team

The team with the last player left is the winner. Then have the teams switch sides and start a new round. If you want to make it really competitive, designate the overall winner as the first team with 10 winning rounds.

BEAN BALL TOURNAMENT

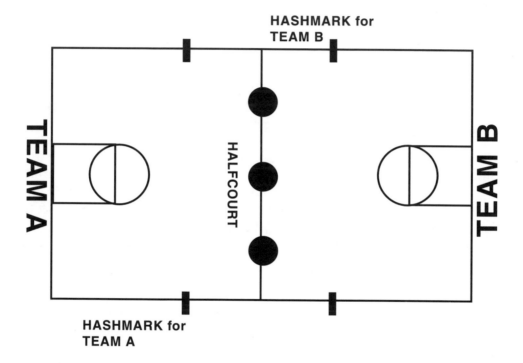

Maze and Tortillas

What's Needed:

☞ a large empty gym or auditorium size floor
☞ paper
☞ pencils
☞ masking tape
☞ kitchen area
☞ supplies for making tacos (tortillas, ground beef, cheese, lettuce, etc.)
☞ unusual taco toppings (cherries, whipped cream, bananas, kiwi, etc.)
☞ plates and cups
☞ drinks
☞ chalkboard and chalk

Description:

This afternoon is rather corn-y. The first suggestion is that you skip lunch and move directly from the session to the activity. There is plenty of food to come!

The first part involves the students in making a walk-through maze out of masking tape on the gym or auditorium floor. Draw an example of what you mean on the chalkboard. Then assign the students to three groups. Give each person a pencil and a piece of paper and have them design a challenging but realistic maze. When finished, have the group leaders collect all the papers and secretly number each one 1, 2, 3, etc. on the maze-side of the paper. Next, the leader puts the papers in the middle of the circle and asks the group to take a vote on which maze they would actually like to design. After deciding, move the groups to the gym or other floor space you have reserved. Give an ample supply of masking tape to each group and have them get to work on each of their mazes. When finished, have the students take turns going through each maze, the first time on their hands and knees!

Part two of the afternoon is a little different, though sure to be appreciated by a group of hungry kids. While the maze making is going on, a leader should brown some ground beef and set out the condiments. When the teens return, have them go through a buffet line to make their own tacos. If anyone is willing to try one of the unusual taco toppings, let the person go for it. If not, serve a fruit salad with whipped topping for desert.

Bike Rally/Movie Event

What's Needed:

☞ one bike, helmet, and lock for every participant
☞ money for movie tickets
☞ parents or parishioners willing to host rest points with refreshments along the way of the bike rally
☞ game items (see below)
☞ one copy of the bike rally map for every participant

Description:

This is a bike rally (not a race) in which the participants follow a predetermined map to the homes of three or four parishioners, where they can play a game and have a simple snack and drink. The final stop of the rally is at the local movie theater where the teens take in an appropriate afternoon feature.

Plan a map from your starting point at the church in a logical order to each of the parents or parishioners who have agreed to sponsor a stop along the way. Give each person a map and remind them to observe all safety rules on the way. At each home, take a break with a short game or activity. (You will need to arrange for all the game items to be at the homes prior to the rally.) Possible activity ideas might include:

First Stop

Play a series of *Twister* games. While some of the teens are playing, the others can enjoy a drink of lemonade.

Second Stop

Divide into teams. Play a few rounds of *Trivial Pursuit*.

Third Stop

Play a friendly version of "spin the bottle." Seat everyone in a circle. The two people the bottle is pointing to exchange compliments with one another (not kisses).

Fourth Stop

Get into the movie theme. Play a game of movie charades where the teens act out famous movie titles or scenes and the rest of the group tries to guess the name of the movie.

End the rally at the movie theater. Make sure to lock the bikes. Then enjoy the movie. (If your group is large enough, you may be able to arrange for a group discount.) After the movie, ride together back to the parish where parents can meet for pick-up.

Halloween Fun

What's Needed:

☞ several pumpkins and knives

☞ paper bags with different kinds of "edible" objects; for example, carrots, peppers, a pickle, a hard roll, and candy

☞ makeup kits to decorate the faces of those not in costume

☞ a large collection of candy to be distributed to children

☞ tissue paper in which to wrap the candy

☞ addresses of children in the parish (optional)

☞ Halloween snacks and drinks

Description:

This is a combination of a Halloween party and service event. Begin and end with the "party" portion.

Have the teens wear masks or full costumes. Hold a few Halloween contests and play some games. For example, divide the participants into small groups of three or four for a pumpkin carving contest. Tell them to allow input from everyone in the group and then go to work on their masterpieces. Award several prizes like "scariest," "ugliest," "cutest," and "sloppiest" jack-o-lantern.

Continue in small groups. Distribute the makeup and have the participants decorate the faces of anyone not in costume or mask.

Next, the service portion begins. Have the participants wrap candy in tissue paper for distribution to younger children. Go with the group (in costume) to distribute the candy to nearby homes with young children, the homes with children who are members of the parish, the children's ward of a hospital, a religious education program for younger children, or any other place where children might be and might enjoy this surprise.

When the group returns, play at least one more game. For example, call on volunteers to come to the front and choose any one of the paper bags with an "edible" object. Tell them to close their eyes, reach inside, and take a bite of whatever it is. Obviously there will be some built-in winners and losers in this game.

Conclude by sharing Halloween snacks and drinks.

Haunted House Visit

What's Needed:

☞ money for admission to a local haunted house
☞ transportation to the haunted house

Description:

Throughout the month of October, many organizations create and sponsor haunted houses. Plan a visit to one of these ghoulish places.

You may wish to call ahead and inquire about group rates and also about times when the lines won't be as long. Make sure the teens go into the haunted house with at least one other person. Show them a meeting place outside of the haunted house where you expect them to return after they have finished.

Of course, if your area does not have a haunted house, your group can create and sponsor one itself. Or, work together with a youth program from another church or community organization and sponsor your own haunted house. The stage area of an auditorium is a very adaptable setting. Additions like tunnels through large boxes, strobe lights, costumed monsters, etc., are all proven winners.

Cemetery Tour

What's Needed:

☞ transportation and arrangements made to visit a local cemetery

☞ copies of a prepared questionnaire asking the participants to locate information on tombstones

Description:

This event allows the teens to think more about death, the communion of saints, and previous generations in both their family and community.

Arrange to visit a local cemetery. Give each participant a prepared questionnaire asking them to locate information on various grave markers, for example:

* the person born the longest time ago
* the person who lived the longest life
* the person who lived the shortest life
* a person who died at about the same age that you are now
* an unusual tombstone verse or message
* a person with a first name or surname similar to your own

You may also wish to ask more specific information for the participants to locate, for example:

* the date that Fred Halliday died
* the place where Ruth Frandsen was born
* the verse written on the tombstone of Kerry Stack

Gather the group for a picnic somewhere on cemetery grounds. Have them share the information they discovered and some of their thoughts about death and being at a cemetery.

Autumn Adventure

What's Needed:

☞ arrangements for a hayride
☞ money for admission to the hayride
☞ parents to provide transportation

Description:

A traditional hayride is lots of fun, especially if it takes place near sunset on a cool autumn evening. Many local and state parks sponsor these types of events. Make a call and reserve a spot for your group.

If possible, allow for a stop on the hayride to get out and enjoy the scenery. Offer a prayer of thanks for the abundance of the land and the beauty of the day.

Another option for this event is apple or pumpkin picking at a nearby orchard. Or, you can bring apples and share a snack at your hayride rest point.

If you aren't able to arrange a hayride, take a walk with the group in a local park. Arrange for an adept storyteller to surprise the group, sit them down, and tell them a Halloween story they will never forget.

Video Game Tournament

What's Needed:

☞ at least four televisions with video game hardware
☞ various video game software

Description:

Advertise this event as a video game tournament. Arrange for color televisions to be placed in four corners of the room. Ask teens to supply the video game hardware and their favorite video game software.

Set up the tournament so that at least two people are always playing one game at a time. Keep a notepad and paper at each station. Ask the players to record both their won/loss record in head-to-head competition and their score for a particular game. Rotate the participants from game to game. At the end of the event, award prizes for champions on each game, total overall score, best head-to-head win/loss record, etc.

While the teens are waiting to play the video games, run an ongoing game of charades in the middle of the room. Whisper common movie (*Rocky II*) and television titles (*Sesame Street*) and other portrayable phrases ("Notre Dame wins on a last-second field goal") to volunteers and have them act them out without speaking.

Thanksgiving Scavenger Hunt

What's Needed:

☞ copies of a printed list of packaged food items, especially those that make up part of a Thanksgiving meal such as cranberry sauce, pumpkin pie mix, boxes of dressing, cans of corn and other vegetables, bread rolls, boxes of gelatin mix, boxes of flour and sugar

☞ shopping bags to collect the food items

☞ a list of addresses of parishioners (optional)

Description:

A Thanksgiving scavenger hunt for food items can be combined with the collection activity suggested with the Thanksgiving lesson (page 147) or for any lesson in November.

There are two main ways to handle the scavenger hunt. One that works very well is for the teens to hang bags with a letter explaining the project (e.g., where the items will be donated, who they will benefit, the kinds of items needed) on the doors of various homes in the area. The letter should also tell when the teens will return to pick up the bags with the person's donation. In conjunction with this method, the teens should approach the managers of local grocery stores to solicit the store's donation.

A second way to run this project is as a regular scavenger hunt in which the teens are given the list of needed items and asked to go in pairs or small groups through the neighborhood or to designated parishioners to ask for any items they have on hand. You may wish to award a prize of some kind to the group that brings back the most items.

ABOUT THE AUTHOR

Michael Amodei, currently an editor of adolescent curriculum materials at Ave Maria Press, was a junior high school teacher for many years at St. Monica Elementary School in Santa Monica, California. He also served as director of religious education and youth minister at St. Monica's.

A recent columnist on youth ministry in *Religion Teacher's Journal*, Amodei has authored and collaborated on many religious education projects, including the *Developing Faith* series (Ave Maria Press) and *Marriage and Life Choices* (Benziger). He has a Master of Arts in religious education from Loyola Marymount University.